P9-CJQ-346

LISTENING TO GOD IN TIMES OF CHOICE

THE ART OF DISCERNING GOD'S WILL

GORDON T. SMITH

InterVarsity Press
Downers Grove, Illinois

©1997 by Gordon T. Smith

All rights reserved. No part of this book may be reproduced in any form without written permission from InterVarsity Press, P.O. Box 1400, Downers Grove, IL 60515.

InterVarsity Press® is the book-publishing division of InterVarsity Christian Fellowship®, a student movement active on campus at hundreds of universities, colleges and schools of nursing in the United States of America, and a member movement of the International Fellowship of Evangelical Students. For information about local and regional activities, write Public Relations Dept., InterVarsity Christian Fellowship, 6400 Schroeder Rd., P.O. Box 7895, Madison, WI 53707-7895.

Scripture quotations, unless otherwise noted, are from the New Revised Standard Version of the Bible, copyright 1989 by the Division of Christian Education of the National Council of the Churches of Christ in the USA. Used by permission. All rights reserved.

Cover illustration (photograph):

ISBN 1-56865-477-4

Printed in the United States of America

This book is dedicated
with much love and respect
to my wife,
Joella A. G. Smith,
a woman of discernment.

"Many waters cannot quench love,
neither can floods drown it."
SONG OF SOLOMON 8:7

Foreword

The art of discernment is of renewed importance for committed Christians, both Catholics and Protestants, today. I say "renewed" because discernment is central to the vision of Christian living in the epistles of St. Paul and in the first letter of John. It also played a prominent role in the thought and writing of the fathers of the church and many of the saints and theologians of the church's first millennium. Gradually, however, discernment gave way to a hierarchical or authoritarian model of divine guidance—with the result that discernment became the preserve of those in church government, who told the rest of us, the community, what God wanted us to do; and of spiritual directors, who performed the same role for their individual, submissive directees.

What occasions our change of emphasis today? Why are we newly aware of Paul's and John's (and Jesus' own) stress on a *personal* listening to the Lord by the individual Christian? As Gordon Smith points out, this is not a new concern, even in the modern, postmedieval church. John Wesley and Ignatius Loyola (and, to a lesser degree, Martin Luther and John Calvin) are our ancestors here.

But as Gordon also notes at several points, the insights of these great reformers of the sixteenth century have perhaps been more honored in the breach than in the observance. There has been what George Lane would call (in *Christian Spirituality*) a "second-generation phenomenon": the institutionalization by these reformers' successors of a great religious charism—Wesley's by the Methodists and Ignatius's by his Jesuits.

This is nothing new, of course. The Pharisees were criticized for the same reason by Jesus himself, and there can be little doubt that the second-generation Methodists and Jesuits, by and large, were devout and sincere people. But we do have to note the deviations if we are ever going to be able to recapture the original spirit of discernment.

Gordon Smith is in the Wesleyan tradition (he is a minister and a college/seminary administrator in the Christian and Missionary Alliance, currently academic vice president of Canadian Bible College and Canadian Theological Seminary in Regina, Saskatchewan). He discusses the way Wesley has been institutionalized in the "fleece method" and the "blueprint approach" to discovering God's will for us.

His primary purpose, however, is not to criticize but to recapture for us the spirit of discernment so central to John Wesley— and to Ignatius Loyola, whom Gordon compared to Wesley in his excellent doctoral dissertation at Loyola School of Theology in Manila, Philippines. This he does in a way both solid and eminently practical. What he has to say, and the language in which he says it, will speak especially to his Protestant fellow believers.

As I write this, though, Gordon and I are coteaching a five-day seminar on discernment at King's Fold Retreat Center in Cochrane, Alberta, near Banff. The mornings are "Catholic" and the afternoons "Protestant"! Since it is now afternoon, I am listening as he discusses chapter seven of this book and appreciating again how solid, and solidly practical, his approach to discernment is. We have come a long way since we first met in 1984, when I taught him courses on discernment and apostolic spirituality in Manila. In this book he witnesses to the positive impact on his life and vision of my "father in the Lord" as a Jesuit, Ignatius Loyola. I, in turn, have been greatly enriched by the Wesleyan Reformation perspective Gordon is sharing now with the seminarists at King's Fold—and shares with you in this book.

For me, at least, this is ecumenism at its best: each of us shares out of the riches of his own tradition, his own grasp of the mystery of Christ. We do not "water down" or compromise our own vision, but like the Buddha's blind men describing the elephant, we are immensely enriched by hearing from others—others who are touching other parts of our infinite elephant—and can thus enlarge our own "vision." Whatever your Christian tradition may be, may you be similarly stretched by your encounter with Gordon T. Smith.

Thomas H. Green, S.J.

1

Dancing with God

Do not quench the Spirit.
Do not despise the words of prophets, but test everything;
hold fast to that is good; abstain from
every form of evil.

May the God of peace himself sanctify you entirely . . .
1 THESSALONIANS 5:19-23

Decision-making is part of life. We face choices big and small every day. And every day the decisions we make shape our lives and the lives of those we love. We know that through our choices we make a difference.

We make decisions at home—purchasing a house, moving from one home to another or making renovations to our houses. We make decisions about family—whether it is education, major expenditures, health care options or how we will respond to a crisis.

We make decisions in our work, whatever our call—whether we are in the gospel ministry in a church-related vocation or whether we are in business, the arts, the civil service or education. We make a decision when we accept a position, when we are in the midst of an important work-related choice or when we are wondering how to respond to a critical issue with a colleague, whether to hire or fire someone, or whether to resign in the midst of a conflict.

At home and at work, we make decisions constantly and know that in these situations we need the wisdom of God and a sense of God's direction.

I could go on—beyond home and work—for the act of choosing is something we are doing constantly, in every dimension of our lives. And we do not live well unless we choose well. We do not follow Christ with integrity unless our decisions and choices reflect that commitment.

Deep within each of us is a desire to choose well—to do what is right, to act in wisdom, love, truth and justice. We long for this in part because we fear the consequences of poor decisions. But we also long to please God, and we long to do what is right for those we love and those we serve. And the only way we will rise above our potential for foolishness and misguided choices is to learn to make decisions well.

Therefore, the capacity to make a decision well, to choose wisely and confidently, is a fundamental skill for Christian life and ministry. Few things are so crucial as evidence of spiritual growth and maturity. People who consistently make poor choices suffer as a result, and they do so unnecessarily. The provision and guidance of God are there to help us; we have the words of Holy Scripture and the wisdom of those who have gone before us in the history of the church.

The sense of vulnerability in times of decision is accentuated for those who live in cities. Amid the busyness and noise we live from one day to another bewildered and confused by the array of choices that are forced on us. Discernment is a critical skill, especially for urban Christians facing many competing and demanding opportunities each day. But discernment is also necessary because we are so transient. The average urban dweller moves every three years. We face changes in our employment, in our place of residence and in other aspects of our lives. Our only hope for sanity is if we can in some measure know that we are able to speak with God, hear the voice of our loving Shepherd amidst competing voices and know that he is guiding us.

It does not make sense for a Christian to live in constant anxiety, worrying over whether the right decision has been made or paralyzed by an inevitable decision. We cannot live in a straitjacket of indecision; neither can we live continually second-guessing choices we have already made. If we are to live with inner peace and sanity in this perplexing world, we must be able to make choices with confidence and live in peace concerning those decisions. And surely the Bible is clear that our God longs to guide us and give us an assurance about our tomorrows. Surely as Christians we should be able to live with confidence, for we are called to live in communion with the living God.

This is why developing the art of discernment is essential to Christian maturity. But as with any art, time and patience are required if we are to learn and master the craft. Discernment comes with growth in wisdom and maturity. Just as children need the guidance of parents, new Christians need the guidance of more mature believers as they grow up in their faith.

Different Views of Divine Guidance

Recently, at least in evangelical circles, two perspectives on divine guidance have competed for acceptance among believers. I will be looking at these more fully in chapter seven, but it may be helpful to identify them both now in order to be clear about my own approach to this subject.

Blueprint school. The first might be called the "blueprint" approach. This perspective sees God as having a perfect plan or blueprint for each person's life. In determining the will of God, the focus is on external signs and counsel that help the individual determine God's perfect plan or purpose. Those who take this approach assume that there is one and only one perfect plan for each individual and that this perfect will can be discovered by an examination of signs, or what are often called "open doors."

My concern with this perspective is that it seemingly undercuts a central conviction of mine—and a central emphasis in this book: the presence and voice of God in the times of choice. The contrast will be immediately evident. I will be suggesting that in a decision we certainly need counsel, and we certainly need to examine our circumstances, but most of all we need to listen to God.

Wisdom school. A second perspective that has gained acceptance in recent years focuses on the wisdom God grants to Christians. In his book *Decision-Making and the Will of God* Gary Friesen provides a compelling critique of the blueprint approach to divine guidance. He goes on to affirm that God does not expect his people to look at signs and open doors, or even listen to little voices in their heads. Rather he believes that through Scripture the Christian's mind is renewed. Through immersing ourselves in the scriptural revelation we develop and grow in wisdom and become increasingly capable of making good choices.

A Response to These Perspectives

These two views, though seemingly opposite, cause me a similar discomfort. It seems to me that in both cases God is distant from the decision-making process. The "blueprint" people look for signs and examine circumstances. The "wisdom" people essentially trust their own capacities to make choices. But somewhere in all of this we must ask about God. And there is a whole stream of Christian thought that has consistently affirmed that in times of choice we can and must listen to God. God is present; God does speak; and we can, if we will, hear and respond to his prompting.

Some reject this notion outright. They have seen the idea of God's speaking to people abused in any number of ways. They have heard people attribute questionable actions to a voice in their mind. We Protestant Christians usually retreat and affirm that we must listen to the Bible. Catholic Christians, on the other hand, tend to affirm that we should listen to the church. Both groups say that we cannot trust a subjective impression; rather, our only hope is to depend on an objective witness, be that the Scriptures or the church.

But is this not an overreaction? Is there not a distinct sense throughout Scripture, and evident in the lives of many believers throughout the history of the church, that God is indeed present when we are facing times of choice? The Bible affirms from beginning to end that God is a shepherd to his people. And a shepherd guides. It is appropriate for Christians to sing, in the words of the great Welsh hymn, "Guide me, O thou great Jehovah, pilgrim through this barren land." The world is daunting. The choices we face can be very confusing. But we are not alone. God is with us at each moment of our lives, particularly those critical decision-making times. Many individuals described in the Bible but also innumerable people in the history of the church have had a specific, direct encounter with God and an assurance regarding his purposes and will.

Abraham was to leave home and head for Canaan. The young Samuel said, "Speak, for your servant is listening" (1 Sam 3:10). We even have the example of God speaking through a donkey (Num 22:21-23). In unique situations in the history of the people of God, God chose to speak very specifically. And God continued to speak. If we examine the lives of the apostles, we find plenty of cases illustrating this immediate work of the Spirit. The whole of the book of Acts gives testimony to a remarkable sensitivity to the voice of God directing, guiding and prompting. Philip was led by an angel to a road south of Jerusalem, where he encountered the Ethiopian. Paul was led to Damascus and to Ananias through a word from God. And Peter, in a dream, was advised to go to the house of Cornelius. The church in Antioch (Acts 13) was directed to set aside Paul and Barnabas for apostolic service. Direct, specific guidance was given throughout the public ministry of Paul. Sometimes the apostles ran from danger, as in Thessalonica; at other times they were impressed by the Spirit to stay on and preach despite the danger, as in Corinth (Acts 18).

But a question still remains for some: Can we as twenty-first-century urban Christians also know clear direction from God? If we can, it is only because of Pentecost. It is only because the Spirit of God has been granted to the church and to each individual believer. The Spirit rebukes, corrects and convicts of sin. The Spirit consoles, comforts and brings encouragement. And the Spirit guides and directs and reveals the mind of God.

Some people have made exaggerated claims regarding God's guidance. They trivialize the guidance of God by claiming that God has provided them with specific directives regarding innumerable situations. They speak constantly of the Lord telling them this or that. We weary of this and may be tempted to react with skepticism. But the abuse of this tremendous gift from God—the voice or prompting of the Spirit—cannot lead us to abandon this provision.

I write out of a conviction that we can know the mind of God, not merely in a general sense, but in a specific, existential sense for the choices and decisions that shape our lives. Later I will respond more fully to other perspectives and reservations, but my basic contention is that we can meet, know and listen to God. I do not suggest that there is a blueprint, a perfect plan for our lives that we need to discover and follow. I recognize the limitations of this perspective and will address it. But questioning this perspective does not mean that we are left to fend for ourselves. Rather, we live and act as men and women who have the option of personal and intimate communion with the living God.

Friendship with God

So when and how does God speak? Are we to live waiting for direct messages from God? We can affirm that God does provide specific words for his children at the critical moments of their lives. But these words from God in specific situations are not the norm—not even for those who are described in Scripture as receiving what was a direct word from God. If we live constantly looking for these directives, we soon begin to trivialize or abuse the gift of God's presence and voice.

What we need, then, is a model for understanding the context and basis for God's guidance in our lives. The most helpful place to begin is with the principle of *friendship with God.* We have the potential for a unique, personal and dynamic relationship with God; and it is from this relationship—not as servants, but as friends—that we can encounter and respond to God and his will.

This means two things, at least. It means we are not left to our own wisdom; but also this model suggests that when we seek the mind of God, we are not blindly following orders. We meet God as followers and friends, as men and women whose desires, wills, personalities, problems and relationships matter. They matter, that is, to God. He meets us as Lord and friend. Our meeting with God is the meeting of two wills, both free.

Yes, at times the will of God has been communicated in a manner that was astonishing because it was so specific. But in the biblical narrative the primary concern of each recipient was communion with God, not specific directives from God. Not only does God speak to his children, but he does so from the remarkable vantage point of a friend. Discernment and guidance do arise from the meeting of believer with God. God does speak to us. But God encounters us as friend, as one with whom we have communion and fellowship. It is this perspective of friendship with God that can provide us with a meaningful model for discernment and guidance.

As friends of God we know that God can and does speak with us. But we also know that we are encountering the sovereign God in the mystery of personal relationship, and we dare not overstate the nature of that friendship or how specific the guidance of God has been. We cannot abuse the gift of God's presence and voice. Nevertheless, we can confidently affirm that God is with us and speaks to us.

The turning points of our lives, our times of decision, are opportunities to meet and know God more deeply and understand ourselves more fully. This self-knowledge arises from an encounter with God. We do not come alone to the crises of our lives. We come as men and women who walk with God. We know God and live in the security that he knows us. We do not meet God as equals. God is God. But we do meet God as free persons who are invited by God into fellowship with himself.

This understanding of discernment and guidance is subtle and complex. There is no neat will to discover; it is not just a matter of applying principles to life. There is a personal, intimate relationship—a reality that may seem to cloud the issue. But this is also liberating. We act before God and with God as men and women who are transformed by encounter with God. Our lives are lived out of this encounter. And this gives energy and joy to our daily experience and to the process of making decisions.

Implications of the Discerning Friendship

This understanding of discernment and guidance carries certain important implications.

1. Discernment relates to the whole of our Christian experience, not just to an isolated segment—a time of decision. Our life in its entirety must be lived in response to the Word of God. Discernment is the word within the Word of God—the specific word to us as individuals, but as individuals who seek to know and live by the Word. We cannot isolate a particular decision from the rest of our lives in order to seek God's guidance. Ernest E. Larkin puts it well in his insightful book *Silent Presence:* "Discernment can never be successfully carried out if it is only an occasional act that is foreign to one's usual total life. We discern as well as we live, and we live as well as we discern."[1]

I am an integrated person. Any decision I make must be considered within the context of my whole life. My objective, then, is not just to discern at crucial decision-making points, but *to be a discerning person.* St. Paul speaks of being transformed by the renewing of our minds so that we will be capable of discerning the good and perfect will of God (Rom 12:1-3).

2. This approach also presumes that discernment arises out of our prayers. Our friendship with God is sustained in prayer, and it is in prayer that we encounter the will and purposes of God and allow God to speak to our wills, our motives, our desires and our priorities. Nothing is so critical to our spiritual formation than the nurturing of our prayer.

3. This understanding of discernment, and of our relationship with God based on friendship, assumes that we do not approach our encounter with God purely pragmatically. We often speak as though God has only work for us to do, and that if we talk to God he will give us more work, more responsibilities and probably some business we would rather not do. Such a perspective is a

consumerist distortion of God. For the Lord, relationship comes before accomplishment. Discernment, then, is the opportunity to deepen the relationship so that our actions in the world arise out of communion with God. God's will and love for us are not utilitarian. He does not love us for what he can get out of us. He loves us for ourselves. He loves us as we are, for he created us. He calls us friends.

The model of friendship with God assumes the phenomena of two wills and two freedoms, God's and mine, in continual interconnection. But my response to God, and particularly to the will of God, must be a response of submission. We are friends of God, but we are not equal with God. The will of God must of necessity have priority. God is God. Our Christian experience is lived in submission and response to the love and will of God.

But the will of God is not arbitrary or autocratic. It is comparable to the actions of the lead partner in ice-skating. In ice-skating, as in any form of dance, there must be a leader. One partner leads, the other follows. The one who follows is not passive or limp, but eagerly engaged in response. There is give-and-take, point and counterpoint. The one who follows exercises a personal will in the dance. The lead skater does not drag the other across the ice. Rather, the genius of the dance on ice is that as one leads, the other follows in full response. Both are fully engaged.

Discernment, indeed the whole Christian experience, is like a dance with God. God in his love and holiness invites us into a dialogue, a conversation, a relationship that includes not only submission but also the engagement of our will and our freedom with God.

In our finitude and mortality, though, we also recognize that there are certain limits to the act of discernment. Many are completely convinced that God speaks to his children. But those of us who readily accept this inner witness need to appreciate the limits of our assurance or confidence in a word from God. It could be that we have overstated or trivialized the voice and prompting of God. We will never have absolute certainty regarding anything we do, other than what is morally right or wrong. As Larkin stresses, discernment gives us only the inner assurance that we are acting "in the Lord." It assures us only that the Lord is in what we are doing and that our hearts and minds are acting out of a deepening encounter with God. Our discernment does not lead to absolute, infallible and irrefutable answers, but only to an assurance that we are living and working in response to God.[2] Yet this is the very confidence we seek. We move in peace because we are dancing with God.

Learning from the Masters

Wise Christians learn from the masters. As we seek to develop the art of discernment, we learn from those who have gone ahead of us. They will help us make sense of Scripture. But more, they will help us understand our own experience.

Many points in the story of the church could be instructive for us, but throughout this reflection on discernment I will make regular reference to four particular moments or times in the history of the church, each helpful in a different way as we seek to understand the art of listening to God in times of choice. First, the insights of Martin Luther and John Calvin are very significant as they wrestled with the issues they faced in their leadership of the Reformation. Second, I will draw heavily on the perspectives of Ignatius Loyola, who in many ways is a unique authority on discernment. Then also, I will note the insights of John Wesley, who broadened considerably the church's understanding of the inner witness of the Spirit. Finally, I will look to authors of the last century, including two out of my own spiritual tradition,

A. B. Simpson and A. W. Tozer, as well as others such as Thomas Merton and Thomas Green.

The experience of these different authors is noteworthy, even though it is far from infallible. Those who have preceded us have made mistakes; they learned by trial and error. But their pilgrimage is invaluable for us as we appropriate their wisdom and insights in our response to the biblical text. In many respects I see this book as an attempt to bring together the accumulated wisdom of those who have preceded us.

One more note before I conclude this opening chapter. The focus of this study is personal discernment. I fully acknowledge a need for a reflection on corporate discernment, particularly in the life of the church. We can and must learn to recognize the footprints of the Spirit in the life and witness of the Christian communities where we worship. My premise, though, is that we learn to discern within the church and in the world by *first* learning to recognize the presence, work and voice of God in our own lives.

2

Seeking the Best

And this is my prayer, that your love may overflow more
and more with knowledge and full insight to help you to
determine what is best, so that in the day of Christ
you may be pure and blameless, having produced the harvest
of righteousness that comes through Jesus Christ
for the glory and praise of God.
PHILIPPIANS 1:9-11

Discernment *is a discriminating choice between two or more* competing options. It is an act of judgment. Usually discernment pertains to those times when we are forced to choose. We marry or we remain single; it cannot be both. We will attend this university or the other; it is not possible to attend both simultaneously. We must make a discriminating choice. Within the context of Christian faith, discernment is a critical reflection in faith and humility that enables us to more fully be disciples of Jesus Christ and fulfill the call to be men and women of love.

Different Kinds of Decisions
It is important to recognize that not all decisions are of the same nature. First, there are times of choice when we can have no doubt of the intent or will of God. Ignatius Loyola, for example,

speaks of occasions when a person is so powerfully illumined by God's presence and grace that there is no doubt of God's intent. Ignatius points to Paul and Matthew as individuals who were not seeking the Lord and were not even disposed necessarily to God's will, yet became aware of the will of God in a manner that could not be doubted (*SE* 175).[1] In such cases discernment is not necessary; the experience is dramatic and intense. As Ignatius notes, these are rare moments that cannot be sought; they are the exception, and they are sheer gift.

Second, Ignatius explains that there is another set of choices that requires no discernment. In these times we feel calm assurance that we are to trust our own judgment and make a good decision through the exercise of reason (*SE* 177). The majority of our decisions are actually made in this fashion, and this is not a less-than-Christian or less-than-appropriate way to make a choice. We do not live with little voices in our heads telling us what to do at each question mark in the day.

A. W. Tozer, a spiritual writer within my own tradition, also affirms that not all decisions are of the same kind.[2] He stresses, of course, that some matters require no discernment because Scripture is explicit that something is either true or contrary to God's Word. But Tozer also notes that on some occasions God "wants us to consult our own sanctified preferences." He believes that in the majority of our daily decisions God expresses no choice "but leaves everything to our own preference." The cloud of uncertainty that many Christians feel about their decisions, Tozer says, arises out of a failure to see that God has given them the freedom "to follow their own personal bent, guided only by their love for Him and for their fellow men." Tozer stresses that this kind of decision-making is not inherently less spiritual. We actually honor God by exercising our judgment and even our preferences.

It is yet another set of decisions that will be the subject of this book. As Tozer notes, for some kinds of choices Scripture is not explicit, and we are forced to choose between two good options. In these situations we recognize that much is at stake. It is then that we turn to the Lord and seek the wisdom of God, with the assurance that God grants wisdom to those who ask (Jas 1:5-6).

In these times of choice, when we turn to the Lord and seek divine wisdom, we need to learn how to listen. Usually these are the decisions that shape our lives and determine the course of our future and those of our loved ones.

In a book on spiritual mentoring Tad Dunne makes a helpful and clarifying distinction between *basic* decisions and *instrumental* decisions.[3] Basic decisions include matters of vocation, whether we should marry, whom we should marry, what our basic lifestyle will be, whether we will speak out against a certain injustice, whether we will join a church or resign from a position. Basic decisions establish the criteria, the set of values, the direction or parameters of our lives. Instrumental decisions, on the other hand, involve the *means* to fulfill basic decisions. When instrumental decisions become too complicated, or too many, or too confusing, we need to make some basic decisions regarding the focus of our lives and our priorities.

The following discussion will be guided by this perspective. Basic decisions are fundamental to our lives, setting direction and priority and establishing the values by which we will live. It is these decisions that will be the focus of our reflection. How can we make basic decisions that reflect the will of God, respond to God's love, best reflect who we are and who we are called to be, and, finally, represent where we can make a difference in our world?

Seeking the Best

The language of the apostle Paul in Philippians 1:9-11 gives us a point from which to consider the nature of spiritual discernment. His prayer is that his readers be able to determine or discern what is *best,* for in so doing they will become pure, blameless and fruitful. Thinking of discernment as "seeking the best" places us on a very helpful vantage point from which to appreciate the nature of the decisions we face. There are several reasons why this is helpful.

1. *Discernment is a discriminating choice between two or more good options.* Paul's words remind us that discernment, at least as I am using the term in this study, is *not* a discriminating choice between good and evil. We are not considering whether to abide by the moral will and commandments of God. Where good and evil are set before us, we do not need to discern. We are called to avoid evil and do good. Discernment in these circumstances is not needed; we need only to obey.

Discernment is the task of Christian believers who are resolved to do good and only good. The challenge is to discover what is best in a given situation and opportunity. We are choosing between two or more good options. Good or evil is not the question; rather, the challenge is to know what is *best.*

When we speak of what is best, the assumption is that when we seek the best, we are seeking that which glorifies God. But more, it means that we are seeking what is best for us as individuals or as a community. And what is best in God's eyes will also be what is best for us. For God seeks what is good for us. God longs to satisfy the desires of our hearts. God longs to see us flourish and do well; when we do, he is glorified.

2. *Discernment honors previous decisions and commitments.* Discernment seeks the best in light of previous irreversible decisions and commitments. We seek to know what is best in such a way that we honor the vows we have made—for example, the vow of celibacy or the vow of marriage. If we have children, we have

another irrevocable commitment. Perhaps we are carrying debts that must be repaid. So we discern in light of all such responsibilities, duties and social obligations. God does not expect us to violate these fundamental commitments or the promises we have made.

We listen to God explicitly and precisely out of the context of our life, not in a vacuum. And God will in the end speak to us specifically within the context of our real situation—not some ideal or fabrication, not what we wish our life were but what it actually is.

The principle of honoring the past applies also to a broader range of noncovenantal obligations. Because God is not capricious, we probably should have a certain bias against change. Recognizing that we may be prone to run from trouble or from difficult relationships, we should generally assume that God will want us to maintain our obligations and fulfill contracts rather than abandon commitments. Of course we may be called to break a contract. However, our bias should be against change. Discernment honors the past—the decisions and commitments we have made.

3. *Discernment always seeks what is best for today.* Discernment enables us to see the new possibilities in even the most difficult of situations. We will never be freed to discern what is best unless we are prepared to accept both the limitations and the opportunities that are part of our situation.

Humility demands that we accept our limitations, and sometimes those limitations may seem severe indeed. We cannot redo history; we can only accept the present. We cannot fix the past; we can only begin again today.

This will mean accepting our own foolishness and mistakes. The past is gone, and given our sin and error, we confess our wrong, turn from it and begin again. There is no need for self-recrimination. That will only mire us in the past and accomplish nothing. Today is a new day, and we need to start over. The mistakes of the past have consequences for today, but the grace of God allows us to face today as a new day and discern what is best now, despite the mistakes of the past.

Recently I read a book by Reynolds Price, American writer and professor of writing, who tells of his encounter with spinal cancer and his road to healing. He had been a healthy, strong and virile man. After his recovery from cancer, he had to accept that he would now be a paraplegic. What I find so impressive about his story is that his healing was in part sustained by his refusal to be caught in the trap of self-pity. To be healed he had to get beyond regrets about the past and, rather than being sorry for himself, persist in gratitude.[4]

Seeing the possibilities of our present in light of our past also means accepting the past actions of others. Perhaps you had the potential to be an Olympic athlete, but an accident caused by a drunk driver left you with crushed limbs. However horrible and tragic that event, discernment means seeking the best in light of that past. Forgive. Mourn the loss. But then move on and seek what is best now. And in God the best is always a new day, a new opportunity. If we are willing to open our eyes and see, the new opportunity will invariably be a sign of the goodness and grace of God. For the grace of God is always greater than sin.

This does not mean that past mistakes and the evil of others are to be denied. I do not make light of the pain we experience— not for a moment. I am only saying that it is useless to lock ourselves emotionally into the pain of the past. That would keep us from seeing the opportunities of today and the potential for tomorrow. Each day is a new morning with God, a new opportunity to know God's grace and respond with hope. We start fresh with this moment, this day and this week.

H. D. McDonald used to speak of God as the great Innovator. The genius of God is the ability to bring grace, goodness and opportunity out of even the darkest of circumstances. Conditions may be difficult and tragic; but if we are open to the grace of God, we can experience hope and goodness and be the means by which others will know this grace as well.

Sometimes the pain of the past is not the result of sin or wrongdoing. Some suffering just happens. Joni Eareckson Tada is well known as having endured terrible suffering as a result of a recreational accident that left her a quadriplegic. No one was at fault. What has made Joni remarkable is the way she accepts her limitations and is able to see the opportunities for today within the context of the past. Discernment requires an acceptance of the past and the limitations of the present.

We can stop saying "If only . . ." and agree that there will be no regrets. We learn from the past, but then we consider today and tomorrow and discern what is best in light of our limitations and opportunities. God is greater than anything that has happened or could have happened.

A Portuguese proverb says it well: "God writes straight with crooked lines." The great Innovator has an incredible imagination, and grace is greater than our sins or the sins of others. God can indeed do immeasurably more than all we can ask or imagine—and God is so great that he can do this within the context of any situation.

4. *Discernment is not a matter of curiosity but of decision.* I need to stress that discernment is not something we dabble in. We are not seeking to know for the sake of curiosity, or to see if we like the results so we can decide whether we will do what we discern. Such an approach violates the very purpose of discernment and violates our relationship with the Lord. So the assumption I make is that discernment is a matter of *decision*. We regularly come to

crossroads great and small where we must make a decision for our sake, for the sake of those we love, for the well-being of the church or the organization we serve.

And we wish to make our decisions as discerning people. Discernment is for decisions—so that our actions can be made with inner peace and confidence.

5. *Discernment is an individual and conditional matter.* Discernment is distinctly personal and conditional. On the one hand, this means that we cannot discern for other people. What God tells one person may not be the same as what he says to another.

A wealthy young man came to Jesus and asked what he should do to inherit eternal life. Jesus told him, "Sell all that you own and distribute the money to the poor; . . . then come, follow me" (see Lk 18:18-25). In the very next chapter of Luke's Gospel we read of another man, Zacchaeus, who also was wealthy—and his wealth was acquired by unjust means. The rich young ruler was a good man, and we can assume that he acquired his wealth through just means; Zacchaeus was a corrupt government official. Yet it is notable that Jesus seemingly says nothing about Zacchaeus's wealth, at least nothing that is recorded. This tax collector responded to Jesus with a concern for justice and a tremendous expression of generosity. Still, his largesse came to only half of his wealth. His word from the Lord was different from the one the rich young ruler received.

Even in similar circumstances God will lead one person or group in one direction and another person or group another way. You are seeking what is best for *you* in *your* situation at this time and in response to the call of God on *your* life. Discernment is profoundly personal and individual. There is no tidy, neat manual on how to live the Christian life, applicable to all people in all circumstances.

This is particularly so with finances. Many Christians would love to believe that God requires 10 percent of our income and the remainder is ours to do with as we please. But such a perspective fails to recognize that all of our wealth is God's. *All* of it. Some may be called to give 10 percent, but some may be called to give 90 percent. Some may be called to give it all away—every last penny.

When we formulate simplistic rules about giving or any other aspect of the Christian life, we cut the vital cord of communication between the believer and God. We need to be determined to discern for ourselves what is best in our situation; but more, we must entrust one another to God. We cannot judge one another or assume that God will lead others in the same way he has led us.

The other side of this is that we need to be freed from the oppressive judgments or expectations of others that limit our ability to hear and respond to God's voice for us. In some cases these pressures will mean that hearing and responding to his voice will be a matter of courage. The reality is that we live in social groups, even Christian communities, where others want to control or influence us. Sometimes the desires of parents keep their children—their *adult* children—from freely hearing the voice of God. Sometimes the desires of pastors hinder the members of their own congregation from recognizing the prompting of the Spirit. Thus St. Paul urges his readers not to "quench the Spirit"—or, in the words of another translation, "Do not put out the Spirit's fire" (1 Thess 5:19 NIV).

We need counselors and advisers; I will stress this more in chapters to come. But a good counselor or adviser is always a catalyst that enables us to hear God well so that we can know what God wants for us.

Distinguishing the Voice of God

To discern is to distinguish the voice of God from the noise of this world and the false witness of the Evil One.

To do this we need to remind ourselves again and again that God is eager to respond to and guide his children. He is Father, Shepherd and loving King. He does not leave us stranded but willingly answers when we cry out for wisdom and guidance. The epistle of James assures us that God is the giver of all good gifts, and this includes the gift of wisdom. If we are in doubt, we should ask for wisdom (Jas 1:5, 17). God does not abandon us in a time of decision.

It is important to stress this because we will often feel the absence of God at the critical junctures of our lives. Many times God will seem silent, and we may think we have been deserted. We are children and God is our Father. But he is the Father of adult children. In times of decision the motives that drive us and the faith that nourishes us will be tried. God could give us simple answers; he knows what is best. But as adult children we discover that he often keeps a gentle distance, providing us with the necessary space to discern and in the process to mature in our faith.

God may indeed seem absent, but in those times when he seems to be elsewhere he is probably nearer than ever. He does not abandon us. And through the times of uncertainty we must remind ourselves that God is eager for us to know and do what is best. He does not toy with us or keep us in the dark for some perverse reason. We must remain confident in this: God loves us and wants our best.

Yet knowing that God wants to guide us does not in itself give us the direction we seek; we need to learn how to recognize his prompting. We may be well-intentioned in our conviction that the Lord loves us and will guide us, but we must still develop the spiritual art of discernment.

For the Old Testament believer, discernment primarily involved discriminating a true prophet from a false prophet. God spoke and communicated his word through the prophets, but false prophets abounded, whereas true prophets were rare. It was necessary that the people of God be discerning in order to hear and respond to the prophets sent from God.

The New Testament believer also needs to be discriminating, learning to discern false teachers from true instructors. But the critical act of discernment for us is recognizing the witness of the Spirit. We are enjoined to test the spirits (1 Thess 5:21, 1 Jn 4:1). This includes distinguishing authentic preaching from false (2 Cor 11), discovering the prompting and guidance of the Spirit in organizational decision-making (Acts 13:1-3), and recognizing the inner witness or prompting of the Spirit.

We live now in the age of the Spirit. According to John's Gospel, Jesus advised his disciples that he would leave them, if only for a time, and assured them that he would return. In his absence he would send another Counselor, a Comforter, to be with them. He would send the Spirit of God. The Spirit would guide them into truth; the Spirit would convict of sin. Recognizing the prompting of the Spirit, therefore, is essential during this period between Christ's departure and his return.

The Witness of the Spirit

But how are we to understand this prompting? The classic reference to this has been the expression "the inner witness of the Spirit," and for Protestant Christians the great spokesperson for this inner witness was John Wesley. Wesley spoke of the inner witness of the Spirit as part of his overall affirmation of the priority of the heart. His basic assumption was that true Christianity is rooted in a heartfelt encounter and response to God. His perspective was profoundly shaped by his own experience, and nothing in his experience was so formative in his religious development as a time when his heart was "strangely warmed"—a phrase he would come to describe as a God-given assurance of his acceptance in Jesus Christ.

But Wesley lived and preached in an era that was suspicious of anything that threatened the rational on the one hand and the visible, hierarchical authority of the church on the other. In a rational age Wesley could not live his confession down. He was accused of being a fanatic, an enthusiast, because he believed that the Christian believer needs to experience a direct witness of the Spirit. He was roundly criticized and ostracized by the church leaders of his tradition (Church of England). They argued that authentic faith is ultimately rational—that the beginning and end of faith come in one's understanding, in rational conviction. That the Holy Spirit could reveal himself personally—bringing a word from the Lord—to a common believer was an idea that Wesley's bishop, Bishop Butler, found abominable and thus inconceivable. For Butler all the Christian needed was to be found through the logical teachings of the church.

Wesley admitted that there is a real danger in acknowledging a direct revelation from the Spirit. He saw the possibility of fanaticism and that people would presume to know the voice of God. But he also believed Scripture, and his Christian heritage taught that the individual Christian can know the witness of the Spirit. He built his whole doctrine on this matter around the pivotal expression of St. Paul: "the Spirit [bears] witness with our spirit" (Rom 8:16; see also Gal 4:6). This concept assumes a union of spirits, Wesley believed, wherein there is harmony and understanding. The validation and primary expression of this union is joy, the joy of creature in union with its Creator, of child with Father. Wesley describes this witness of the Spirit as "an inward impression on the soul, whereby the Spirit of God directly witnesses to my spirit, that I am a child of God; that Jesus Christ hath loved me, and given himself for me; that all my sins are blotted out, and I, even I, am reconciled to God."[5]

For Wesley this confidence that we are loved and accepted by God is essential and foundational to the rest of our Christian experience. We cannot mature in faith, grow in love and be men and women of hope unless we have an assurance granted us by the Spirit that we are children of God, accepted and forgiven by the Father. Wesley, then, begins here.

But he goes further. He believed that the Spirit also "shines upon his own work, and clearly shows what he has wrought." That is, there is a continuous, ongoing relationship with the Spirit. Christian believers can have the assurance that their spirit is in union with the Spirit of the living God, as the basic and most elemental fact of their existence. To be a Christian, for Wesley, is to be in fellowship or union with the Spirit.

Vital to Wesley's doctrine at this point is his firm conviction that this inner witness of the Spirit will always have an outward expression. A test of this experience and inward knowledge is essential. Wesley himself notes, "How many have mistaken the voice of their own imagination for this witness of the Spirit of God, and then idly presumed they were the children of God, while they were doing the works of the devil!"[6]

Consequently Wesley stresses that two signs give evidence of the union of Christian believers with the Spirit. The first is *confidence,* an assurance that we are children of God. The second is *character,* a moral transformation that is the fruit of union with the Spirit. Wesley often quoted 1 John 2:3, "By this we may be sure that we know [God], if we obey his commandments."

Joy and a desire to do good and turn from evil might summarize this verification of the inward reality. Inward joy and confidence that we are children of God must be accompanied by moral reform. The one without the other is not enough evidence. Joy without moral transformation is mere sentimentality; moral transformation without inward joy is mere morality, not true religion. Joy with a desire to turn from evil to holiness is the essential stance as we discern the feelings and voices of our conscience and make sense of the fellowship we have with the Spirit.

For Wesley, then, the heart is important to our Christian experience. The inner consciousness of the presence of God is critical to our spirituality. The central feeling or emotional state is joy, which for Wesley is a consciousness that the believer is a child of God, an awareness that brings assurance of personal identity with God, security with God and acceptance by God.

God desires to direct and guide us. But he can do so only if we are discerning men and women, growing in our ability to recognize and respond to the prompting of the Spirit. We will fail, certainly; we will sometimes confuse the voice of God with temptations from the Evil One or with longings that arise from nothing more than our own pride or selfishness. We will make mistakes. But if we are resolved to know and do the will of God and determined to seek and do the best, we will surely grow increasingly in tune with the Spirit of God. It may take time; spiritual maturity does not come overnight, and neither do wisdom and discernment. If we persevere, however, we will become discerning people.

Recognizing the Prompting of the Spirit

We need to learn how to listen, how to recognize the inner witness of the Spirit. Our task is to grow in our recognition of the prompting of the Spirit. We do so best when we recognize that there are four distinct messages that we receive from the

Spirit—four different ways the Spirit prompts the people of God. First, the Spirit assures us of the love of God. Second, the Spirit convicts us of sin. Third, the Spirit leads us into truth. Fourth and finally, the Spirit guides us at the decision times of our lives. It is of utmost importance to stress that we cannot learn to recognize the prompting of the Spirit in the fourth area, in times of decision, if we do not learn first to respond to the prompting of the Spirit in the first three areas.

First, Scripture tells us that *the Spirit witnesses with our spirit that we are children of God* (see Rom 8:16). This is foundational. If we are not assured of the love of God, we cannot make choices confident of the guidance and direction of God. When John Wesley had a profound experience at Aldersgate Street, the root of this encounter with God was an assurance that his sins were forgiven and he was accepted by God. We must, like Wesley, know we are loved, forgiven and accepted. There is nothing more foundational to the Christian life and nothing more basic to spiritual discernment.

Second, in the description of the ministry of the Spirit in John 16 Jesus emphasizes that *the Spirit convicts of sin.* The Spirit calls us to repent of sin and turn from evil. We must remember, though, that not all feelings of guilt come from the Spirit. Some guilt is self-imposed—when we fail to live up to our own expectations. Some guilt is that of the Evil One, who condemns us for sin we have already repented of. And some guilt comes through the judgments of others—as often as not a false guilt. The only guilt that is redemptive is that which comes from the convicting ministry of the Spirit.

And again, unless we learn to respond to the prompting of the Spirit with regard to sin, we cannot learn to hear the voice of God in our times of choice.

Third, the Spirit, we read in John 16, *leads into truth.* We can learn to listen to the Spirit's voice by being a people who intentionally respond to the initiative of the Spirit of truth. The Spirit leads us into spiritual illumination and understanding. Without a commitment to truth, we cannot expect to hear the Spirit of truth in our times of choice.

These three, then—assurance of love, conviction of sin and guidance into truth—are all foundational for those who would learn to respond to the prompting of the Spirit in times of choice. They cannot be bypassed. The chapters that follow will focus on the prompting of the Spirit when we face a decision. But we learn to recognize the voice of the Spirit by first responding on the three prior levels.

The Priority of Prayer

Before we examine further what it will take to listen to God, though, we must affirm something fundamental to this whole process: discernment arises out of a personal encounter with Christ, specifically the encounter of prayer. We can be discerners only if we are pray-ers. We discern the voice of God within the context of a relationship. If that relationship suffers, so will our ability to discern what is best. Our first and foremost task as we seek to discern is to learn how to pray, how to meet with God, delight in his presence and know him.

The same expectation applies to any relationship, actually. If an individual wants another person to inform her choices and shape her decisions, and if she is eager to have that person share wisdom and insights with her, then she must attend to that relationship. She will nurture the friendship, get to know the person, so she understands and can appreciate the perspective that person brings. She will delight in opportunities to be with this friend. It is the same with God. We must, then, learn to pray and make our prayers, our communion with God, a priority.

But it is not enough to emphasize the importance of prayer. This needs to be *listening* prayer. For so many prayer is talking to God rather than communion with God. It is one-way communication—either asking things of God or keeping God informed of what is happening in the world. Discerning prayer requires that at times we simply shut up and remain silent in the presence of God. This may take time to learn if we are accustomed to dominating the conversation with God, if we are used to setting the agenda with him.

Further, we do not pray in isolation from our activities in the world—our problems, conflicts, opportunities and work. Thomas Green speaks of discernment as the critical bridge between prayer and our activity in the world. We pray as men and women who are keenly attentive to what is happening in our lives and our world. We pray as those who live in the world, bringing all that we are and wrestle with to our encounter with God. But more, from our prayer we return to the world as men and women informed by the encounter with God.

It is discernment that enables us to live fully and freely in the world, able to respond to opportunities and situations, able to seek the best and live peacefully with the decisions we inevitably must make. As discerning men and women, we are fully engaged with our world—freed from the oppression of the past, freed from regrets for our mistakes or the actions of others, freed to see hope and new opportunities. We are freed to fulfill our vocation.

3

The Personal Foundations of Discernment

I appeal to you therefore, brothers and sisters, by the mercies of God, to present your bodies as a living sacrifice, holy and acceptable to God, which is your spiritual worship. Do not be conformed to this world, but be transformed by the renewing of your minds, so that you may discern what is the will of God—what is good and acceptable and perfect.
ROMANS 12:1-2

When *it comes to discernment and effective decision-making there are no shortcuts. There is no simple method of finding God's will or making easy decisions. Discernment, even for those practiced in the art, can be a very trying spiritual experience.*

The principles of discernment are clear and can be learned by any sincere Christian. But there are some key foundations to a discerning life that we can never take for granted. The outline of the personal foundations for discernment that follows will lead us to reflect on elements that are foundational to the Christian life as a whole, but we will be examining these from the perspective of the matter of discernment.

As we will see, these elements are never complete in our lives. We can never check off these items as though they lay behind us.

All three are ideals for which we long. Each, though, is an essential element in the personal foundation of our lives if we are to discern well.

As noted, there are three—at least three. And in significant respects they arise out of the words of the apostle in Romans 12:1-2. The Scriptures call us to present our bodies as living sacrifices, holy and acceptable to God. Further, we are called to be transformed by the renewal of our minds. *Then* we will be able to discern what is good and acceptable to God. *Then* we will be able to discern what is the best.

The Fundamental Commitment

Our only hope for effective discernment is clarity in our allegiance. Whom do we serve? What is our first loyalty? Can we appreciate the call of Scripture to present our bodies as living sacrifices to the living God?

Paul's reference to our bodies is a call to present all that we are and have—the whole of us, soul and body, mind and emotions, hopes and aspirations—to God. We offer the whole of who we are as living beings, alive and longing for life, filled with hopes and dreams. All these things are part of the living sacrifice we offer to God.

Spiritual masters of every era in the history of the church have recognized the primacy of this question, the matter of our fundamental commitment. Ignatius of Loyola, for example, stresses that in a time of choice, when we listen to God, the basic question is one of allegiance. In the *Exercises* we read, "In every good choice, as far as depends on us, our intention must be simple. I must consider only the end for which I am created, that is, for the praise of God our Lord and for the salvation of my soul" (*SE* 169).

Nothing is so critical to discernment as one's basic disposition or attitude. Ignatius sees this stance as a matter of loyalty to Christ and the cause and values of Christ. The central question is our willingness to do the will of Jesus and our commitment to the glory and kingdom of the Lord. Effective discernment is dependent on allegiance to Christ.

Thomas Green adds the following insight. This commitment to Christ must include a measure of passivity or "openness" to God and the purposes of God. A religious zealot may be piously active but still unable to hear the voice of God. Misguided zeal may be mistaken for true loyalty; self-important bustle can easily replace a quiet devotion to Christ.

Ignatius thus sees discernment as taking place in the context of prayer, especially prayer where our loyalty to Christ is affirmed and our motives are purified. The greatest danger in discernment is that our pride and selfish motives will lead us astray. In the setting of prayer we can be honest about our motives and clarify them as we seek to know what is best.

First and foremost, a discerning person is an individual who seeks righteousness and is committed to the glory of God. In chapter two I discussed Philippians 1, noting that discernment is "seeking the best." But also noteworthy in the opening verses of Philippians is the assumption that we seek the best "so that in the day of Christ [we] may be pure and blameless, having produced the harvest of righteousness" (vv. 10-11). What is best, not just good for us, is that which enables us to be a holy people. So we cannot discern what is best unless there is a fundamental commitment to righteousness—that to which this best is ultimately oriented.

A. W. Tozer stresses this same principle. Seeking to provide help to those who wish to know how the Lord leads, he writes, "First, it is absolutely essential that we be completely dedicated to God's high honor and surrendered to the Lordship of Jesus

Christ. God will not lead us except for His own glory and He cannot lead us if we resist His will."[1]

Tozer makes a critical distinction. Some seek to use God—employing God, so to speak, to achieve selfish ends. But we can be discerning people only when we are fundamentally abandoned to the purposes of God.

A Mind Renewed by Scripture

I grew up in a spiritual tradition that stressed the importance of surrender. We were led often in the singing of "I Surrender All," and the general assumption—of which we were reminded again and again—was that our deepest problem was that we were not sufficiently surrendered to God. Our wills were in battle with the will of God, and insofar as we lacked absolute surrender we would surely lack fulfillment and fruitfulness in our spiritual lives. Surrender was the great panacea. If there were problems in our lives, it was assuredly because we were not sufficiently surrendered. "Is your all on the altar?" our preachers would ask.

There was some truth in this call to surrender. I have already noted that critical to the process of discernment is that we clarify our fundamental commitment. But here is the problem: this call to surrender was only half the truth, and as such it was a subtle form of heresy. Our transformation and the process by which we are made discerning people must include a second element, or else the first is meaningless. *We are also called to transformation by the renewal of our minds.* Ironically, the religion of my youth was quite anti-intellectual—stressing verse 1 of Romans 12 but seemingly ignoring the full implications of verse 2, the call for a renewed mind.

Few things are as critical to the personal foundations of spiritual discernment as our understanding of the way we think. As is stressed in Romans 12:2, we are able to discern the will of

God *if* we are being transformed by the renewing of our minds. For this there is nothing so important as Scripture. It is primarily through Scripture that our minds are renewed.

We need to examine the role of the Scriptures in discernment as part of the objective standard against which the subjective witness of the Spirit is tested. All inner prompting we experience is not of God. Not every inspiration we have comes from the Spirit. Thus our inner witness must be balanced by objective realities. At critical points in the history of the church this objective balance has been defined as twofold: the Scriptures and the church. The history of Protestantism is instructive here, for we can draw on how Martin Luther and John Calvin responded to the idea of the inner witness of the Spirit.

Luther had a continuing battle with Thomas Müntzer, whose group lived by daily witnesses from God. Luther's objection was that the group refused to submit to two critical standards of examination: "brotherly conversation" and the Bible. Luther obviously stressed the importance of Holy Scripture, but he also faulted Müntzer for the lack of commitment to spiritual community. True wisdom, Luther insisted, is not divisive but peace-loving.[2] The subjective witness must be balanced by the objective—the Spirit's witness through Scripture and the Christian community. This, as we will see, is the primary contribution of the Reformers to the matter of discernment.

Some recognize John Calvin as responsible for introducing the expression "the inner witness of the Spirit" to Protestantism, if not to Christianity. Though Calvin initially affirmed the reality of an inner witness, he ended up spending much of his public life fighting off those he termed "spiritualists." But his condemnation of these groups came because they failed to be informed by and subject to Scripture. They sought inner illumination, but they ignored Scripture. Perhaps in reaction, by the end of his life and teaching Calvin even began to question the place of private Bible study and to insist that the Spirit speaks exclusively through the preached and taught Word. His hesitancy to affirm that the Spirit can communicate directly to the believer has shaped Protestant churches ever since then, particularly those in the Reformed tradition.

It is unfortunate that Calvin had to react so strongly to the abuse of the "spiritualists." Yet his perspective, taken together with the concerns of Luther, offers a valid lesson: the subjective witness of the Spirit must be balanced by the objective witness of the Spirit through Scripture and in the church. If we neglect Scripture and fail to live in mutual submission within the Christian community, we have no context in which to assess whether the inner witness we have is truly from the Spirit of God.

The role of Scripture is foundational. The Spirit whom we seek to hear is the same Spirit who inspired Holy Scripture. The Holy Spirit, then, does not invent things. He only communicates the Word of God and the will of Christ. Quite simply, if we do not know the Word, we cannot know the mind of God. The communication of the Spirit to our hearts and minds is the specific application of the Word to our lives. This means that we cannot be filled with the Spirit (Eph 5:18) unless we are indwelt richly by the Word of Christ (Col 3:16).

There is no new revelation by the Spirit in the scriptural or apostolic sense. But the illumination of the Spirit is not merely the enabling that helps us understand the Word. It is more than illumination or understanding. The Spirit also prompts, guides and directs the Christian believer. But we can confidently attend to the prompting of the Spirit only if we are men and women of the Word. We can recognize the voice of the Spirit amid myriad competing noises only if our minds have been tuned by immersion in Holy Scripture.

The Spirit will never contradict Scripture. When we are faced with competing options, both or all of which may be good and valid options, what we will long for is communion with Christ by his Spirit. So if we have neglected the study of Scripture, we will be at a distinct disadvantage.

Finally, those whose understanding is shaped by Scripture are also most capable of rightly perceiving themselves and their world. The study of Scripture renews the mind and enables the Christian believer to more fully appreciate the will and purposes of God in the world. This in turn helps us discern what is best at the decision-making times of our pilgrimage.

A Life Lived in Christian Community

The second objective criterion by which discernment is tested, and thus the third element in the personal foundation of a discerning life, is that we know what it is to live in Christian community.

The Reformers clarified the priority of the church or the Christian community. Discerning men and women are members of God's holy church, the community of faith. This does not mean merely that we hold some kind of formal membership in an orthodox Christian church. The intent is much greater. To be discerning people we need to know what it means to be in *spiritual communion* with fellow members of the body of Christ. We should know what it is to live in submission within a community, to all members of the community, but particularly to those in appointed leadership within the church.

A Christian outside of fellowship with other believers is in grave spiritual danger. When we are isolated from community, we are no longer accountable for our insights or actions. We must test our impressions, insights and perceptions. It is arrogance to assume that we can somehow discern on our own whether the impressions we have are God's word to us. We need the check and balance of the community as well as the encouragement that comes from the household of faith. Ideally we should be able to confidently assert that our impressions regarding the prompting or direction of the Spirit are subject to the affirmation of those within the Christian community.

Throughout this study I will be stressing the importance of accountability. We are easily deceived and misguided. Discerning people recognize this and set up checks and balances in their lives. If those to whom we are accountable—whether a small group of peers, a spiritual friend, a pastor or a spiritual mentor—cannot affirm that the impression or word we have received is truly from God, we need to question whether indeed this word is from God. Those who do not live in some form of structured community and spiritual accountability do not realize how easily our pride can deceive us. So if for no other reason but that we are called to live as members of the Christian community, the Reformers recognized and affirmed the importance of the church.

The personal foundation for discernment, then, is made up of three ideals that continually shape not only our growth in discernment but the course of our lives: our fundamental commitment, our minds renewed by the Scriptures and our lives lived in Christian community. Each of these is an essential element in our lives as we become discerning individuals.

4

The Peace of God

God is a God not of disorder but of peace.
1 CORINTHIANS 14:33

*The peace of God, which surpasses all understanding, will
guard your hearts and your minds in Christ Jesus.*
PHILIPPIANS 4:7

N*ow we come to the heart of discernment—the matter of peace.*
Christians who have made a decision often say they feel peace
regarding the choice. Rarely do we question this; we assume that
if they have this so-called peace, there is little more to ask or say.
In this we are both right and wrong. It is true that we seek peace
when we make critical choices. It is in peace that we know or
recognize the inner witness of the Spirit. But peace in and of
itself means little. We are wrong if we don't question ourselves
or others regarding peace, for we need to determine if this peace
is from God.

We come then to an examination of what it means to know
the peace of God in discernment, and for this we need to reflect
on the matter of feelings.

The Insights of Ignatius Loyola

One of the turning points in the life of A. B. Simpson, a spiritual writer within my own tradition, came when he recognized that God does speak to us in the depths of our being.[1] But he stressed that we can hear this "still, small voice" only if we are prepared to listen and wait, being attentive to the very depths of our being. Simpson refers to this as "an old mediaeval message."

At this point we become particularly indebted to Ignatius Loyola, who in many ways is the master of discernment. This Spanish mystic of the Counter Reformation discovered and formulated the essential principles of discernment that apply to Christians of all ages, traditions and cultures. He is best known for his work *Spiritual Exercises,* which includes "Rules for Discernment." These rules serve as guidelines regarding how the Spirit of God functions and the Evil One responds, together with how the human mind tends to work.

Some Christians hesitate to learn from Ignatius, possibly because of his association with the Jesuit order. It is important to remember the following: first, at the time of the Reformation in northern Europe there was a powerful movement of renewal within the Roman Catholic Church in Spain, a renewal that we would do well to appreciate; and second, Ignatius's *Spiritual Exercises* is simply an apt summary of the wisdom arising out of the Middle Ages—wisdom that all Christians need as we seek to know and follow God. His work is an invaluable aid to all Christians who seek to grow in discernment.[2]

In the "Rules for Discernment" Ignatius speaks of different times of choice, but his primary contribution comes in what he calls the "second time" for making a choice—a time when discernment is necessary (*SE* 176).[3] Most often, I believe, his insights pertain to the basic decisions of our lives. Basic decisions, as I explained in chapter one, are those choices or decisions that shape the fundamental parameters and direction we will take, times when we recognize that much is at stake and we are forced to attend to and listen to God.

Recognizing the Place of Feelings

Ignatius's first insight is that discernment is the examination of what is happening in our minds, especially our feelings (*SE* 316-17). He did not for a moment deny that discernment includes a rational consideration of external factors. His insight, though, is that discernment finally rests on internal factors, our inner reactions to external circumstances.

Some Christians think that discernment or guidance is an examination of the circumstances of our lives, a reflection on the "road signs" outside ourselves. But Ignatius, in effect, calls us back to a recognition of the priority of the conscience, the interior of our being. The guidance and counsel of others is important, and circumstances must be considered. But the critical task in discernment is examining what is happening within our conscience.

God does not have a mouth; he does not speak audibly. Rather, God "speaks" to us through our feelings, impressions left on our minds. But we must not equate the voice in our head with the voice of God. We rather discern God's word in the interpretation of these impressions. We discern by perceiving and evaluating the movements of the heart.

In the end it will be reason that guides us—but reason comes to terms with the feelings and impressions that are left on our inner person.

Consolation and Desolation

Ignatius's second insight is that we can generally categorize our feelings in two kinds: consolation and desolation (*SE* 316-17).

These are ancient terms, rich in meaning. Consolation is any feeling of peace, joy, contentment or serenity. It is a sense of well-being, of all-rightness. Desolation is any feeling of anger, depression, discouragement or inner turmoil. Sometimes it may be a feeling of malaise, not a specific feeling or reaction, just inner discomfort or dis-ease.

Ignatius calls us to recognize the potential we have to know ourselves and discern effectively by reflecting on our emotional ups and downs. These are the tender places of our inner lives, where we respond to our recent past, our joys and our sorrows. These are important indicators of who we are.

Naturally, this means we have to be honest with ourselves. We need to be straightforward with what is happening in our minds, recognize where we have failed and feel that failure, notice where there is hurt and disappointment, and acknowledge anger, fear and mourning where these exist. But it also means that we acknowledge our joys, those things that have brought pleasure, gladness, cheer, delight and contentment. Only as we face up to our joys and sorrows can we come to grips with our responsibilities and make mature decisions and choices.

As we gain practice in reflecting on our joys and sorrows, we can assess their significance and recognize patterns and trends. When we move beyond the busyness and superficiality of our lives and become men and women of prayer and reflection, we can truly know ourselves and attend to the impressions and promptings of God. For God is working in us, shaping us through our joys and our sorrows. But we cannot respond to the inner work of God unless we learn how to stop, be silent, pray, think and reflect on this inner work. And reflection, like prayer, is fostered in quiet, when we process what is happening in our lives and attend to our inner reactions and responses to these events.

No Decisions in Desolation

The third insight of Ignatius is that we never make a decision in desolation (*SE* 318). It has been my privilege to have Father Thomas Green help me process most of the critical decisions in my life over the past few years, and there is no more significant counsel that he has given me than this: never make a decision or change a course of action when you are in desolation. Never. Green writes,

> Desolation is the sign of the evil spirit working; thus we should *never* make or change a decision in desolation unless we want the devil as our spiritual director. So important is this rule that I often tell people to remember it even if they forget everything else they ever hear about discernment. If they remember, and abide by, this one crucial rule in their spirituality, they can eliminate 90 percent of the unhappiness in their lives. Good people make bad decisions because they misinterpret desolation, because they take discouragement, dryness, restlessness as signs of God's will for them.[4]

Desolation, in its various expressions, is never from God. God may permit it (as he did for Job and Jeremiah and others), but God never causes it.

Therefore do not make a decision in desolation. Never resign from a position or organization when you are angry or afraid. Do not discontinue a program of study because of discouragement or abandon a time set aside for prayer because of restlessness. At such times we are not emotionally in a state when we can choose well. In desolation we should not change our course of action or make a decision.

This does not mean that we will not feel disappointment in a decision. You may feel profound sadness in deciding to resign from a position or shed tears in making a decision that will cause pain to others but that you know is right. But the decision itself must be made in peace—not anger, not frustration, not in a state of discouragement.

Few things are so fundamental to making good decisions as this principle. Remember that the sign of peace may be the inner strength and courage to make a difficult decision. We read that Jesus set himself toward the cross. He apparently experienced a profound peace and determination to do what he knew he had to do, even though we know, from the Gethsemane experience, that he did not see this as something pleasant.

Recently a friend and colleague put it well when he spoke of a surface turbulence in his life—the turmoil that comes with a difficult choice. He noted that though there was turbulence on the surface, an underlying peace enabled him and freed him to act. We act only in peace; we should make no decisions in desolation.

It is helpful, then, to consider the source or cause of desolation. Ignatius speaks of several sources (*SE* 322): (1) perhaps we have neglected personal responsibility; (2) our desolation may be a trial permitted by God; (3) our desolation may be allowed by God so we might see that consolation is pure grace, not something that can be earned or fabricated.

If we can identify the source of our desolation, we can seek resolution prior to reconsidering our decision. Anger and mourning can be acknowledged and resolved. Where there is sin or dis-ease because of neglect or a lack of discipline, we can confess our sin or sloth and come clean before God and ourselves. If there is no identifiable cause related to sin or neglect, we are simply called to wait on God, recognizing that in the end consolation, God's peace, is his gift. Either way, we do not act or choose in desolation.

On several occasions, full of frustration, I have written a harsh letter to vent my anger. How many times I have been grateful to my wife, Joella, for questioning my action and suggesting that I wait a few days before I send such a letter. Usually I either do not send it or send a toned-down edition rather than a letter that came out of desolation. I inevitably come to regret the angry letters that happen to miss Joella's attention. It never pays to act when our hearts are in such turmoil.

One question that inevitably arises here is what we should do if we are being forced into a decision with no time to come to terms with our heart. When decisions are pressing, it seems we must act; it seems as if life is terribly complicated and demanding, and it would be mere sentimentality to say we have to wait for peace. In such circumstances there is really only one problem involved: we need to go back to the basic, fundamental decisions of our lives. We need to resolve priorities, our guiding life values. We are getting lost in details because we have failed to resolve some basic decisions. At these times it is doubly urgent that we find the space, quietness and distance that will allow us to come to peace. We may even find that the decisions we thought were so urgent are really not so pressing.

Consolation Must Be Tested

Ignatius Loyola's fourth insight is that consolation must be tested. Discernment is fundamentally a time when the consolation of our hearts and minds is tested, sifted and understood. Consolation in itself does not mean that we have the mind of God. Saying that I have peace in my heart regarding a choice does not mean that peace comes from God. I may say I feel confident, joyful and excited about something, but that does not for a moment mean that what I am proposing is good and true and the right thing to do. Is this peace from God? Are the joy and excitement I am feeling attributable to an encounter with God and a directive from the Spirit of God? This consolation must be tested.

Desolation is not from God; it may be allowed by God, but it does not come from God. But consolation may be from God, or it may reflect the deceitfulness of the Evil One, masquerading as good. Or it could reflect our own confused desires and mis-guided motives. It may even reflect nothing more than what we had for breakfast!

Those who recognize that there is an inner witness of the Spirit need to remember that any inner prompting needs to be tested. The fact that we feel we should do this or the other does not mean we have received a word from God. The feeling or impres-sion needs to be tested to discern whether indeed we are acting in a peace granted by God.

Those who deny the possibility of the inner witness of the Spirit often do so because they have seen the excess and abuses of those who attach "The Lord told me this morning . . ." to irresponsible or self-centered actions. Yet the affirmation that there is an inner witness of the Spirit does not mean that *any* inner prompting or feeling is from the Spirit of God. The words of the apostle in 1 Thessalonians 5:19, "Do not quench the Spirit," are followed in verse 21 by the exhortation "Test every-thing."

Ignatius explains that a false consolation may well be attached to what seems noble, honorable and pious. The Evil One will usually not tempt us to do deliberate evil. The Tempter knows that this is ordinarily a less than effective means of attacking the maturing Christian. He is far more subtle. Usually his most successful approach is to persuade the eager Christian to pursue things that are noble, religious and just, things that we know are good in themselves. But the Evil One tries to persuade us to do them for less than honorable motives, or simply to keep busy at something other than what God would have us do.

If a person feels great peace regarding a decision that obviously violates scriptural ideals or mandates, we see clearly that the peace is not from God. It is a false consolation. Remember: discernment is between two or more good options. No discernment is needed in what is clearly not of God. But the Evil One is quite willing to urge us to do something good *if it is not the best.* He succeeds if we accept an assignment, however good, noble and just, that is other than the will of God for us.

If someone says God is telling him or her to evangelize a tribe on the far side of the ocean, or organize a development project or famine relief project for starving African children, or run for president of an organization or a country, then we can properly ask whether the peace is from God. Great causes are quite easily undertaken for questionable reasons. Pious motives have led many to build their own religious kingdoms.

There are two other kinds of false peace that we need to be alert to as well. First, there is the consolation or peace that leads us to accept the mediocre and live within less than our full potential. We sometimes want to avoid the discomfort that comes with change, the tension that arises when we are forced to stretch beyond our comfort zone. So we need to beware of the false contentment that we use to justify being less than we can be.

The second kind of false peace is the temptation to activity and busyness, particularly with administrative detail, for one or more self-centered reasons. For some, preoccupation with busyness and administration are a way of evading the real issues of life; sometimes the demands of work are an excuse to avoid the responsibilities of family, study or prayer. As an administrator, I also know I receive much more personal affirmation when people see me busy doing things that they appreciate. But this could mean that I am neglecting to delegate and thus neglecting some of the essential responsibilities of my work.

This is why the topic of discernment is addressed to *mature* Christians—those who want not only to do good, but to do the good that they are called to do—that which is not merely good, but the best *for them*. And this kind of clarity in our lives, the assurance that we can respond to a call, make choices and act in a peace that comes from God, requires quietness, prayer and discernment.

As will be stressed, a discerning person has learned to question his or her own motives and recognizes the possibility of self-deception. Few things are so humbling as the recognition that our noble ideals may be inspired by the Evil One or our own misguided motives. It is humbling, certainly. But it is far better to discover our vanity and pride *before* we act than after. In discernment, then, we test consolation—our peace, joy and enthusiasm. We find out whether our euphoria or excitement for something—some ideal, some project, some decision—is truly of God.

Ignatius Loyola gives specific guidance on how consolation can be tested. We ask ourselves, What is causing the consolation or peace that we feel? That is, we examine the setting in which we experienced the consolation and determine whether that which caused or inspired the peace or consolation is good, honorable and true. Does it reflect motives that are pure and committed solely to the glory of God?

Ignatius also speaks of consolation without preceding cause. By this he means that we can experience a peace or joy that is clearly unrelated to any external event or inner awareness or thought. There was no word of encouragement from a friend, or insight gleaned from Scripture, or positive development in our work. With no preceding sensory cause, we knew consolation—a deep peace or joy. These experiences may be rare, but for Ignatius and many others they are no less real. In such cases the consolation or peace is truly of God. Discernment is not needed.

Most consolation, however, has a recognizable cause. For example, we were moved during the playing of a favorite symphony or the singing of a great hymn. Or through the words of a sermon or the encouragement of a friend, our faith was strengthened and our hope restored. In these cases the cause of our consolation or joy is obvious. But as discerning people, we need to probe deeper. Ignatius's insights here are particularly helpful (*SE* 333). He suggests that we must be thorough and examine the *beginning,* the *middle* and the *end* of our thoughts or impressions. At each point in the spectrum we should be able to affirm that our intentions are true, our motives are pure, and our purpose is solely to seek the glory of God.

Thomas Green, an expositor of Ignatius Loyola, reminds us that the Evil One is a deceiver and conniver, and that thorough discernment will allow us to discover his presence. Green writes,

> In general, we may say that the devil will always reveal his presence by desolation. He cannot fully mask this presence, nor can he produce a consolation which is genuine throughout. However much he mimics God in the peace and joy of consolation, the tail of the snake will always be evident to those with the eyes to see and the patience to scrutinize their experience.[5]

Zeal without knowledge can be destructive. Great inspirations without careful discernment can be equally harmful. Patience to reflect, consider and confirm that our peace and joy are truly of God is essential. It takes time; we must be thorough.

Green's reference to "the tail of the snake" echoes the language of Ignatius, who speaks of a serpent's tail. It is a vivid image, and a helpful one. As we examine the beginning, the middle and the end of our consolation, if our peace is not from God, the evidence of the Evil One, the "tail," will be evident at some stage of our reflection.

Green suggests the following approach to thinking about the three points in the spectrum.[6] The beginning would be the context or setting in which we were motivated to pray or seek the mind of God. Were we where we were supposed to be, or were we in prayer while neglecting our basic responsibilities and duties? That is, the very context or setting of our prayer and discernment needs to be true and good.

The middle of our thoughts or consolation would apply to our actual time of prayer. Assuming that the beginning or context is good, are the motivating thoughts rooted in humility and service or in vain aspirations and thoughts of anger, discouragement or fear? If in our prayer we are self-righteous, proud of our work or character, imagining the great things we could do for God, or if we are despising others, envying others or feeling the heat of anger against others, then surely our peace is not from God.

Finally, the end of our prayers or consolation, Green suggests, is that which we are prompted to do. What are we inclined to say or do? Where does our peace lead? Is this end good, or is it less than good? Does it end in that which is noble and true, or does it lead to something that violates biblical ideals?

Here we need to go further. If the end is clearly evil, then the tail of the snake is evident. But sometimes we need to remember that the end may be good in itself, but not good for us as individuals. It may not be the best for us in light of our vocation, our commitments or our abilities. I may think, for example, that the end for me is to conduct a symphony orchestra. While in itself this is a noble ideal, I immediately recognize that this is not the best for me in the light of my vocation. It is not evil in itself, but it is not a "good" end for me. (Of course I hope I would already have seen the tail of the snake in discerning the "middle" of my consolation: if I was thinking that I was to conduct a symphony orchestra, my vanity and grand personal aspirations would be more than sufficient evidence of a misplaced tail!)

Another way to look at the beginning, the middle and the end would be to see the beginning as the actual source or cause of our peace, joy or consolation. What is it that brought us encouragement and hope, or an aspiration to do something? Is this cause something that we can identify as good and noble— something that would please God? In this case we could examine the middle by considering our attitude in prayer toward ourselves and others. Do we have feelings of anger, resentment, envy, jealousy or frustration as we consider our peace? Or do we sense any fear or discouragement, or any indication that we want to run from a problem or avoid a difficult unresolved situation? Finally, the end would be the actual thing we believe we are called to do. Is this end noble and good, and clearly something that would please God?

If the consolation or peace that we feel is not from God, the evidence that it is not will surely appear at some point in the spectrum. If this happens, we should distrust the whole experience. As I noted above, we may be embarrassed and disappointed with ourselves when the tail of the snake appears. At this point we know that we were deceived and misguided, usually by our own vanity and confused motives. But it is far better to find this out early than late. And there is no reason to be hard on ourselves or punish ourselves. Having recognized the false consolation early, we can be thankful for the mercy of God and the reminder that the Evil One cannot deceive believers who are prepared to take the time to discern. We can thank God for keeping us from falling prey to our own conceit and misguided zeal.

The Question of Motives

I have made several references to motives, whether misguided or pure. The matter of our motives is of fundamental importance in the task of discernment. We assess our consolation and determine if our peace is from God by reflecting on our motives, three in particular: the desire for honor, the desire for wealth and the desire for security. Each of these can cloud the issues we face and disable us in the task of discernment.

Effective discernment demands that we know ourselves and are honest with ourselves, particularly when it comes to the values that drive us. Deep within we all desire recognition, plenty and security. This should not surprise us. We are created in the image of God and thus have significance and worth. We have been granted the privilege of life in God's world and were created to enjoy God's world. And we are vulnerable, dependent creatures. Where we go astray is in presuming that worth comes through the esteem of others and the honor they show us; that enjoying God's world requires money, the more the better; and that we can gain security by covering all possible openings where we feel vulnerable. Our focus is misguided, for ultimately our only hope for honor, joy and security is found in God. If we seek God and his righteousness, these things will come in their time. The danger is seeking them as ends in themselves, apart from God.

Therefore it is essential to a mature spirituality and to effective discernment that we test our motives, clarify what values are driving us, particularly at the critical junctures of our lives, and turn back to a life that is ordered toward the love of God and his glory. Each time of decision can be a time of spiritual growth, precisely because we are once more forced to reconsider our motives. It is humbling to discover that the pursuit of honor or the desire for financial security may have crept into our thinking and perhaps has come to dominate the center of our thoughts or our prayers. A time of decision calls us back to the fundamental choices we have made and the centrality of Christ in our lives.

Recognizing then our capacity for self-deception, we need to check our motives thoroughly. There should be others in our lives who have the freedom to question our motives—spiritual friends, mentors, pastors; later I will take this up further. For now, the point is that we need to make a self-evaluation in light of the consolation or peace that we are feeling. As we examine the beginning, the middle and the end, we are wise to do so in terms of the motives that could be shaping our thoughts.

Be ruthless with yourself. Your only hope for making good decisions lies in a determination to make them solely in terms of the glory of God and your love and obedience to God. Loathe even the possibility that a decision could be made on the basis of questionable motives. Each of us is capable of rationalizations—justifying our actions, persuading ourselves that our intentions are honorable. We must, then, be resolved to clarify our motives.

Determined to make a decision in truth, we can examine the beginning, the middle and the end with the same care and scrutiny with which a dentist examines teeth. My dentist is thorough. As I sit back with my mouth gaping, he takes his metal tools and peers into every possible space where a cavity could be forming. He misses nothing; he knows that he serves me well only if he goes at my teeth from every angle. While he is doing his job I'm helpless, hoping that he will find nothing wrong, hoping also that he will soon stop and let me go with a blessing and an assurance that there are no cavities. But I know, for my own well-being, that if he is not thorough he is not a good dentist.

Approach the beginning, the middle and the end of the peace you are examining with the same determination. Recognize your potential for self-deception. Acknowledge that your motives are often misguided. We can easily find self-justifying ways of sanctioning our desires for honor, wealth and security. And so for the beginning, then for the middle and then for the end of the peace you feel, ask yourself honest, probing questions regarding motivation. Only then are you being fair to yourself, and only then can you be sure that discernment is truly happening.

A Qualified, Conditional Peace

In closing, I need to add an important qualifier. We see through a glass darkly (1 Cor 13:12 KJV), which means there will always be an element of uncertainty in our choices. In this life we will not have absolute, unambiguous peace and rational certainty that we have divine guidance.

In part this is due to the very nature of human existence. We are creatures, dependent and finite. Our knowledge and understanding will always be limited. The future is hidden and uncertain, and we simply do not know what tomorrow will bring.

The presence of sin in our lives complicates matters further. What makes discernment so difficult is that we can never really trust ourselves, especially our motives. In this respect Calvinists tend to be pessimistic. John Calvin emphasized the severity of the human predicament, noting our propensity to sin, and his followers tend to conclude that it is highly unlikely that we will ever know the mind of the Lord. Wesley and his followers, on the other hand, tend to be more optimistic. Wesley's experience of a warmed heart and the Methodist affirmation of the inner witness of the Spirit have led many to conclude that we can know with certainty the voice of God.

Discernment is most effective where there is a healthy balance between a Calvinist self-suspicion and a Wesleyan self-confidence. We see through a glass darkly, we are sinful, and our motives are never pure. On the other hand, we have the assurance of our Lord that he will be our Shepherd and the promise of Christ that the Spirit of God will be with us and in us. But even if we avoid the extreme of saying that sin negates the possibility of discernment, this tension leaves us with a recognition that we will never have absolute certainty. Even though we affirm the possibility of discernment, of an inner witness of the Spirit, the knowledge of our limitations and the presence of sin in our lives should keep us humble. Further, it should keep us from introducing our comments with "The Lord told me this morning . . ." Even when we have discerned and examined ourselves with utmost care, the most we can conclude is that we have peace that this is the direction we should go; this is the sense we have, which reflects our best efforts to discern.

By not overstating our certainty, by qualifying our statements and not making absolute our sense of divine guidance, we are not negating for a moment the presence and witness of God to our hearts. We are merely affirming our own human limitations and humbly accepting our potential for self-deception. Though we know we are filled with the Spirit of Christ, we also know that we still bear fallen flesh. None of us has pure motives; we are all capable of self-deception. And at different stages of our lives there are different aspects of our hearts that come to the light. But though our motives are never pure, we can determine whether the choice we are forcing is driven by our misguided motives or by the desire to glorify our heavenly Father.

Another thing to remember when it comes to the peace we are granted is that we discern conditionally; we cannot presume upon other people or institutions. Say God leads you to apply for admission to a university. This neither obligates the university nor implies, if you are denied admission, that you did not communicate well with God in making the application. If you feel a peace to apply for a position, then that is what the peace is for and you should not overstate its significance. God in this case is not necessarily leading you to go to that particular university but merely to apply to study there.

This same principle applies to other situations. There are few things so presumptuous as a pastoral candidate's statement that he believes he is called to a particular church. He may have peace about being a candidate, but most Protestant churches require that a group, either in the local church or in the denominational administration, decide in the end whether or not a candidate is assigned to a particular congregation.

There has been an element of doubt and uncertainty at each of the critical decision-making points in my life. But when I have done what I felt was right, with a peace granted by God, the affirmation and confirmation of that decision came later. At some point we trust God and make our choices despite the lack of absolute certainty. We cannot wait until every question is resolved before we act.

The point here, though, is that we are not wise to overstate the significance of the peace we have discovered. It needs to be qualified; we need to affirm its conditional nature.

Yet despite this lack of absolute assurance, we can have peace and thus enough confidence to be able to act without continual second-guessing. We can have a wise confidence in our ability to examine our motives, seek the peace of God and think through our options. We can make decisions before God that reflect his good and perfect will and are the best for us and those we love and serve.

Scripture is clear in assuring us that the God of heaven has a covenant relationship with his people that includes assurance of his guidance, direction and wisdom. He does not leave us orphans; he does not leave us to our own devices or wisdom. He is a friend. The Spirit is called the Comforter and Counselor who is with us forever. We can have this assurance: if we will take the time to wait on God and honestly examine ourselves and our motives, we can know the peace of God that surpasses understanding, and our hearts and minds will be guarded in Christ Jesus.

5

An Intentional
Approach to
Decision-Making

Beloved, do not believe every spirit, but test the spirits
to see whether they are from God.
1 JOHN 4:1

Discernment is an art. It cannot be learned or acquired by reading books, but only by experience, by doing discernment itself. Discernment, then, is not a matter of technique, something that can be learned from a manual in three easy steps. In part this is because discernment cannot be objectified. It is simplistic, then, to tell someone just to pray about something, with bland assurance that God will guide. God does not respond to prayer like a push-button machine. Neither do we. We discern as we grow in wisdom. Discernment itself is very much a process.

But though discernment is an art, something we master as we live through times of decision, there is great value in approaching the task intentionally rather than haphazardly. Christians often fail to make good choices. Usually they do not decide well simply because they are careless or do not take the time to do it well.

There is probably nothing so fundamental to spiritual discernment as the simple principle that it takes time to decide well, and further, that we decide best when we approach our choices intentionally and methodically. Our lives are full of pressures; Christians who live in cities face decisions in the midst of many different demands and expectations. But this is no excuse. We owe careful discernment to ourselves and to God. Our lives are important, and our decisions affect the lives of others. We must find the time and take the time to approach our decisions intentionally. For to discern well we must pay attention: we need to observe and listen, noting what is happening around us and within us and attending to what others are saying.

There are three essential dimensions to decision-making. There are logical connections among the three; in fact, the way I will present them may lead you to assume that there are three steps to the process. But while I stress the need for order and an intentional approach to decision-making, the fact is that life is irregular and complicated. Our emotional response to the options we face can likewise be quite complex. So though I present three stages in the decision-making process, in actual fact we may move from one to the other and back again. These are not three stages or three steps to making a decision, but they are the three elements, and in large measure they do follow one after the other.

It has been my experience and observation that if a decision was poorly made and was later regretted, one of these three elements had been neglected. When all three of these elements are in place, however, there is every reason to choose in confidence and act in the assurance that we have decided well.

Rational Consideration of Options and Obstacles

First, effective discernment does not negate a rational consideration of our circumstances, opportunities, problems, obstacles, resources and abilities. Always be suspicious of the suggestion that we do not need to apply our mind to the issues involved in a decision; this smacks of pious sentimentality or superspirituality. Whether the decision in question is faced by an individual or an organization, there is no substitute for a careful analysis of all that could possibly be involved.

This analysis could involve extensive research. Individuals may need to spend time examining different options as they weigh the pros and cons involved in a choice. Organizations may need to conduct a thorough study of their strengths and weaknesses, their potential as well as their limitations, before a decision is made.

It is good to enumerate and weigh the pros and cons of a potential decision. But it is important in this process to recognize that there are competing values involved in each choice we make. Therefore, as we list the pros and cons, we also need to find a way to ascribe value to them. Even if there is only one "pro" on our list, it may be so significant to us that it far outweighs all the cons.

Individually, we assess our options in terms of our strengths, abilities and commitments. As we consider the possibilities, where do we believe we can make our maximum contribution for God and his kingdom? This consideration needs to be qualified by an examination of our motives, abilities and limitations. But using our mind and our mental capabilities is essential in the process of coming to a good decision. There is nothing inherently more spiritual about an approach governed by the search for the spontaneous or the assumption that God will bypass our need to do our homework.

We can assess in terms of our abilities and strengths as we consider positions in which we might serve. In seeking assurance regarding the person we might marry, we can and must freely consider whether we have a fundamental compatibility with the individual we are attracted to. If we are wondering which of two alternatives would be a more suitable alternative for study, we would do well to see which university or college offers a program that best meets our needs or which institution we could attend most easily. If Aunt Molly lives near university B and is offering free accommodation, then this certainly is a factor in comparisons with university A.

The same need for assessment applies to organizations. If as a local congregation or college or even as a business we are considering alternatives, there is no substitute for planning, research and analysis. Missionary organizations that fail to plan and make decisions in the light of elementary research are naive and presumptuous. For anyone to suggest that prayers and the guidance of the Spirit preclude the need for planning and analysis indicates pious sentimentality, not mature spiritual wisdom. God has given us minds and abilities, and God expects to lead thinking people.

In the end God may lead us to do something that is humanly speaking inadvisable. In a business, we may choose the less profitable alternative. Perhaps we choose to attend a university where we do not have free accommodation, though it was available elsewhere. Still, God does not normally violate seasoned human judgment and the wisdom of years. In Acts 6, the individuals who were to join the apostles in the ministry of the Jerusalem church were to have two qualifications—they were to be full of the Spirit *and* wisdom (v. 3). There is no substitute for thinking, planning and the application of wisdom.

There is another facet to this careful thinking side of effective decision-making: a consideration of the obstacles and problems we are facing or are likely to face. Again, it is an assumed spirituality that either ignores or discounts opposition and problems in our lives and work. We will have obstacles. Recognizing and understanding them is essential to the process of discerning what is best.

In a work situation, we may consider resigning because we think we cannot work with someone who dislikes us or makes our work difficult. We need to acknowledge this reality and face it honestly. Otherwise our discernment will easily be a rationalization that we should resign when really it is merely a means of escape. It could well be that God is calling us to difficult circumstances, to stay in a situation that is highly uncomfortable. I have found it helpful, whenever I have found my life situation difficult, to remember that God's work through his Son involved a cross.

Difficulty in itself, then, does not indicate that we are to resign a position or not choose a certain option. God may well call us to some form of suffering. But we need to discern and be certain that the cross we face is the cross that God is calling us to bear. Thus we need to be open about problems and obstacles. This recognition does not close down the need for discernment. Rather, we bring an understanding of these problems and obstacles into the process of discernment.

For organizations, effective strategic planning includes not only assessment of options and opportunities but also recognition and analysis of limitations, obstacles and potential sources of opposition. We need to understand ourselves well as an organization, our strengths and those things that are not our strengths, if we are to discern well. Problems in the social environment or context in which our organization performs its task must be acknowledged and understood.

Again, this does not mean that if there is opposition or financial limitation, a decision is de facto already made. It merely means that we will discern with our eyes open. When St. Paul faced persecution in Iconium (Acts 14:1-7), he fled to Lystra, where he continued to preach. But in Acts 20:23 he indicates that the Spirit testified to him that he would be facing persecution and imprisonment; in this case, rather than flee, he went openly, and apparently with few if any reservations, to Jerusalem. The difference was entirely one of discernment.

A contemporary example might be a missionary organization that is seeking to conduct ministry in a town or city. The project may prove fruitless; there may be outright opposition. Does the missionary team stay or go? It depends. The fact of scant response to the ministry or the fact of opposition needs to be acknowledged and discussed, but this does not preclude the need for discernment. God may well lead a team to stay for many years, if not the whole of their career, in a setting that is seemingly bearing little fruit.

A lack of financial resources may lead us to accept certain limitations; on the other hand, we may discern that God is leading us as an organization to do something for which there is currently no financial provision. If so, we need to act with a profound degree of trust in God and his provision. The fact of limited resources does not in the end determine the outcome. Rather, we need to face the problem or limitation honestly and allow it to be a factor in the discernment process. In acknowledging limited financial resources, we need to discern whether God is calling us to live within those limitations or to act and trust him for his provision beyond what we currently have. Neither is necessarily better. It takes just as much faith to live and work within strict financial limitations as it does to act anticipating and depending on additional provision or income.

Once while serving on the executive committee of a mission organization in the Philippines I was part of a discussion about what we should do in the face of significant financial limitations. The typical response, one I had heard often, was heard again. Several indicated that we needed to pray more, trust God more, and eventually, if we had faith, we would have more money to work with. But field director Franklin Irwin, a veteran of many years of missionary service, stated simply that perhaps faith would mean accepting the limited financial resources and living within them, confident of God's ability to act even if we had less money available to us.

Faith may mean accepting limitations rather than assuming that they do not belong in our lives.

So opposition, problems and obstacles need to be openly faced and considered. Otherwise when problems arise an individual or a group may conclude that they did not discern well. When potential or actual problems are openly acknowledged, discernment can take these realities into account.

Not all obstacles or problems are signs that we are to turn away, or leave, or resign. Many times God will call us to walk directly into the obstacles and bear them with patience. God may well call an organization to live and work very frugally. Limited financial resources may be God's way of saying that we need to cut back what we are doing. When this happens, the act of faith is believing that God is God, and that God is doing his good and perfect will within those very limitations, even if (*particularly* if) they are financial limitations.

Further, our prayer and discernment need to be informed by a thorough examination of our situation. Part of good decision-making includes making every effort to consider all alternatives. We need to be thorough, because sometimes we may be blind to an alternative or an option that for some reason or another we would rather not consider.

All of this is based on the simple premise that God speaks to us in the context of our lives—not in a vacuum, not in isolation from our lives, but precisely out of and into the jumble that makes up all that we are and hope to be. If discernment is the bridge between our prayers and our work in the world, then surely we must understand the circumstances of our lives if we are to hear God speak to us. A rational consideration of our life or work situation is an essential dimension in effective discernment.

Extended Time for Prayer and Reflection

The second dimension of the process of discernment is extended prayer and reflection. Most Christians do not decide well merely because they do not take the time to do it—the time necessary for an effective decision. Urban Christians, in particular, live such harried lives that there is little time for reflection, prayer and silence, and consequently little time to attend to the quiet presence of God and the prompting of the Spirit.

Just as there is no substitute for careful reflection on our circumstances, there is no substitute for extended time in prayer and reflection. Discernment takes time and cannot be rushed.

I would suggest that, at the very least, you should take a day for prayer and reflection when you face a critical decision. Find a place where you will be assured of few if any interruptions. Find quiet; find space. Preferably it should be a place of retreat, a place where you are familiar with the surroundings and can relax, concentrate on the Lord and attend to him rather than to the surroundings. Ideally it should be a place where you can be alone—alone enough to lie on your back as you pray, or take an extended walk, or sit for a time to record your thoughts and impressions. It should be a place where others will place minimal or, better yet, no expectations on you. You should not be expected to converse with others or respond to their concerns. This is a time for you to be with the Lord, and it needs to be in a place where people understand this and will leave you to yourself.

Most of all, we need time and distance. We need to step aside for a time and get some distance between ourselves and the issues we are facing—some emotional distance from the pressure we feel to make a choice. But we also need distance from others. Often we feel the inordinate pressure from others to act in one way or another, a pressure that can drown out the voice of the Spirit. And so we need time alone with God.

Following is a suggested order for the day, an order that can be adapted to a longer or shorter period of time, depending on the length of time available to you.

Center and focus. Bring clarity and focus to the day by beginning with a time of worship. In silence or through Scripture reading and the singing of hymns, allow your mind to be focused on God and his grace and goodness.

Thanksgiving. In a time of discernment it is crucial to recognize clearly that God loves us and has been faithful to us. In a time of choice we must come to the Lord with a clear sense of his unconditional love. We need to know we are loved; we need an assurance that we will not approach our choice with the thought of gaining God's love by our obedience.

For this assurance the simple exercise of thanksgiving is most helpful. Review your life and note the evidence of God's faithfulness and goodness. Enumerate his blessings. As you are assured of God's love on the one hand and his faithfulness on the other, you will be freed to hear his voice.

Only in gratitude can we be open to seeing all the options and alternatives to which the Lord may call us. Only in gratitude can we see clearly.

Meditation on Scripture. Whether at this point, or later in the time of prayer, or as part of each segment of the day, take time for extended reflection on Scripture. Allow for a measured time of reading, reflection and consideration of the Word of God. True meditation builds on careful study. You will find that meditation is most fruitful when the text is familiar to you—you have already done your study on this passage and resolved some of the key questions of interpretation.

You may wish to choose an extended text for meditation throughout the day. Or you may choose shorter passages to inform and guide each segment of prayer: an invitation to thanksgiving and an assurance of God's love to begin, followed by a passage that will enable you to enter directly into the resolution and cleansing described below, in turn followed by a text that enables you to rethink your allegiance and fundamental commitment. Either way, allow the Scriptures to play a central role in the time of prayer.

Resolution and cleansing. Honestly acknowledge if you are feeling anger, fear, mourning or a sense of loss. Any of these emotional burdens will cloud your heart and mind.

These will be discussed more fully in a later chapter when we examine things that may block our discernment. But for now it needs to be stressed that since we make our decision in peace, we must in some measure move on from anger, fear and mourning. Anger must be resolved. When we are fearful, we can, in the words of the apostle, identify our anxieties through prayer and intercession and receive the peace of God which will guard our hearts and minds (Phil 4:6-7). And mourning needs to be acknowledged. Where we feel the pain of loss—the grief of death, separation or change—our hearts cannot be healed by the glorious peace of God until we honestly face up to that pain and mourn our loss. Stoically resisting the pain of loss or separation is living a lie. Only as we mourn can our mourning be turned to joy. Only then can we know the peace of God.

But we need more than emotional resolution; we also need cleansing. To hear the voice of God, we need to come clean before him, repent of known sin, confess the error of our ways and receive and appropriate his forgiveness. If we are uncertain of his forgiveness, we will not be free to hear God's voice. We will be continually plagued by a powerful inner drive to somehow try to please God, to atone for our sins through our own efforts. We cannot discern unless we are assured of God's forgiveness.

Finally, resolution also includes forgiving those who have wronged us. We need to be sure that we have nothing against our neighbor, that we harbor nothing against those who have wronged us. A colleague put it well once as we considered a deep, horrible wrong he had experienced. He said, "I have set my sails toward forgiveness." Recognizing that forgiveness may be difficult where wrongs were great, at the very least we can set our sights on forgiveness and begin to move emotionally in that direction. For if we do not eventually forgive, we cannot know the forgiveness and freedom of God.

Confirmation of our allegiance. We can never take for granted the first foundation of discernment (discussed in chapter three), that our ability to discern well and make good decisions is entirely dependent on whether we are clear on our fundamental commitment. We need to come back to the center again and again, make this choice once more and confirm our allegiance.

This avowal can take different forms. For the mature Christian it may be nothing more than a renewed statement of desire to serve God and pursue his glory. For the new Christian confirming one's loyalty may be the most critical aspect of the day. Whom do we serve? What motives drive us? Do we seek God's glory or personal honor, wealth and comfort? Here it is helpful to meditate on Scripture, focusing on the critical matter of choice, allegiance and obedience to God's will. For the more mature

Christian it may be more helpful to use this sector of the day for meditation on the life and work of Christ. This in itself will bring clarity of perspective. But whatever the means or exercise, we must discern with a clear sense that our ultimate objective is the glory of God—we seek first his kingdom and his righteousness.

We could meditate on John 21, allow the Lord to ask us the question "Do you love me more than these?" and consider this question in the face of all the loves of our life—all the things we hold dear. Or we could consider the words of Jesus that encourage us to seek first the kingdom of God, and with this allow the Lord to help us see what it is that most motivates or energizes us. Or we may use the time for a renewal of our baptismal vows.

Silence. Accept silence as a time of listening rather than talking to God. In silence, distractions will come and the mind will wander, but gently, without self-castigation, bring your thoughts back into the presence of the Lord. Believing that the Lord is present, simply be in his presence. I find it helpful to have several periods of silence throughout the day in which I seek to be fully present to the Lord.

In the silence, attend to God. There is no agenda; there is nothing that we need to say to God. We can comfortably enjoy God's presence and delight through faith in the reality of God's love. In silence we can experience what is described in 1 Peter 1:8: "Although you have not seen him, you love him; and even though you do not see him now, you believe in him and rejoice with an indescribable and glorious joy."

Journal writing. At points throughout the day, or in one single session at the conclusion, record the developments of the day. Make note of the impressions, feelings and frustrations that have arisen in your prayers. Use the journal as a vehicle of prayer, not for speaking with self but preferably for communicating with God. What do you sense him saying? Where have you confessed sin or resolved an emotional weight? What impressions seem to be dominating the day? Finally, of course, examine the beginning, the middle and the end of the consolation or peace that you have experienced in prayer. Examine the feelings of the day carefully and with attention to the matter of motives. Attend particularly to the times of silence and the impressions you felt in those periods.

By the end of the day, more often than not, there will be an abiding impression that has arisen from our prayers and extended reflection. Sometimes we will have done nothing more than raise more questions or concerns that need to be clarified. We may need to go back to our responsibilities and do our homework, clarify the options and do some research on the matter we are facing. But usually, if we are open with God, sincere in our desire to attend to his voice and do his will and prepared to be thorough in approaching discernment, a clear and distinct impression will arise out of the day, some measure of resolution to the question we brought to our time of prayer.

There is no guarantee that God will answer. At times God will remain silent, and we will not have a clear sense of direction. But then the word from God may well be that we are to wait and not worry, that we will assuredly know what is best in due time when we need to know. Remember, God is not playing games with us, "playing hard to get" or intentionally making it difficult for us to hear and understand him. If we will seek him, he will be found. If we are willing to take the time to know God and the voice of God, our efforts will bear fruit.

Accountability and Discussion with Others

The decision we make, in the end, is a decision *we* must make. Others cannot choose for us or discern for us. An essential mark of an adult, an adult child of God, is that we take responsibility for our own lives and our own decisions. We cannot abdicate our responsibility even when we serve within organizations that make decisions for us. We must be discerning and act according to our best judgment.

Yet as I have stressed, though we are alone in the decision we eventually make, we do not make the decision alone. Wise Christians seek the counsel, advice, encouragement and direction of others. There are many formats that this can take, a variety of ways by which we can be accountable for our prayers and our decision. But whatever form it takes, we need the counsel of others. Once we have a sense of direction, an impression that we believe is from the Lord, we need to allow others to respond to both the process of our decision-making and our conclusion. It may be wise to allow them to participate in the process as well. They could raise red flags for us early and keep us from getting off track.

One format might be an intentional conversation with a small group of intimate friends. There are few gifts so precious as the counsel of friends when we are facing tough choices, whether personal or vocational, whether matters of faith, family or work. Parker Palmer describes the clearness committee of the Quakers as an excellent model for this dimension of discernment. He notes that if a Quaker couple wished to be married, they met with a group of fellow members. This small group joined with them to pray, asking probing questions and raising issues the couple needed to consider as they faced marriage. Noting that the Quakers have expanded this approach to help individuals with a variety of important questions, Palmer suggests that this model could be adopted by Christians from other traditions as well:

> Behind the clearness committee is a simple but crucial spiritual conviction, without which the practice makes little sense and can even become destructive: Each of us has an

inner, divine light that gives us the guidance we need but is often obscured by sundry forms of inner and outer interference. The function of the clearness committee is not to give advice or alter and "fix" people but to help people remove obstacles and discover the divine assistance that is within.[1]

In other words, the group helps the individual or couple with the decision, but they do not make the decision for them. They approach the question as servants and partners, not as manipulators or controllers.

A group like this should be very clear about their purposes. They will pray with the individual or couple; they will ask questions focusing on motives and values, never judgmentally, but as a way of assisting the one facing a decision; they will ask questions only to help the individual ascertain that the matter has been looked at from every angle and that problems as well as opportunities have been considered. As Palmer emphasizes, members of the group are to ask open, challenging, loving questions, not questions that impose a burden but only those that help the individual clarify the word from God. This is not an interview but a time when friends come alongside to encourage and help.

The second format for accountability is that of the spiritual director, mentor or friend. Such an individual plays much the same role as the clearness committee. A spiritual mentor or director does not discern for us, but with us. He or she is a codiscerner, helping us interpret the inner feelings or promptings of our heart.

As friends or mentors, we perform a great service for another when we listen carefully and prayerfully. We are not judging. We are not making decisions for the individual who has come to see us. We are listeners, and we are listening particularly for any indication that the decision-making process was not good, that motives were not clarified, that the individual was not honest with himself or herself.

At the end of an hour together many individuals have heard me say, "I see no red flags." They have spent the day alone in prayer; they have had a question or matter that they were seeking to discern. And at the end of the day we had a time to debrief. "I see no red flags" is my way of indicating that they seemed to have effectively discerned what they needed to know.

As codiscerners we come alongside, listen and attend to the voice of God with others. We seek to provide an outside, more distant perspective. And if we see "red flags," then in love we need to draw them to the attention of those who have sought our counsel.

When you ask someone to serve as a listener, mentor or spiritual friend, it must be someone who will honestly question your motives. A true friend does not flatter and is not necessarily impressed with your statement that you have received a word from the Lord. A true friend will probe and question. Find someone who will be honest with you, or you are wasting your time and theirs.

Further, a spiritual mentor will endeavor to see a matter from a perspective that you might overlook for one reason or another. Often because of our own experience or background, inner blocks blind us to realities that others can help us see. "Have you considered this, or the other?" the listener may ask. We may need to be challenged to face up to areas of our lives that we would as soon not acknowledge.

The third dimension of discernment, then, is permitting others to respond to the impression we have gleaned in prayer and the conclusion we have come to, even if we still feel tentative about the decision. We allow for comment, input, evaluation and assessment. As we listen to others' comments on the process of our decision, we cannot be defensive. We need to be open and willing to listen.

Those who provide the input need to be capable of providing an objective analysis of our discernment, raising relevant questions without interfering with the process of discernment itself. If a mentor or spiritual friend gets emotionally involved in the decision or is affected personally by the decision, it could be that he or she cannot be an objective listener. It would be difficult for them to disengage from the consequences of our decision in order to effectively help us with the decision. I found, for example, when making the tough decision to resign from a position, that I needed to step outside the organization to find an objective listener, someone not actually affected by my potential resignation. The same need for objectivity would apply to a clearness committee.

So there are three dimensions to the discernment process: (1) rational consideration of the options and obstacles, (2) extended time in prayer and reflection, and (3) accountability and discussion with others. If life were simple, these could be three sequential steps: careful analysis of the situation and the circumstances, followed by a day of prayer, followed by a meeting with a clearness committee or a spiritual friend or director. As often as possible this progression should probably be the basic structure we follow. But at times we may feel confused and in need of assistance from a spiritual friend or pastor. At other times we may need extended time in prayer prior to a rational consideration of our options and obstacles. We may need help from a pastor or spiritual mentor in understanding the obstacles we are facing.

So we need to adapt the structure to our needs and the needs of a particular decision we are making. But all three dimensions of the process should be part of our discernment if we are to choose and decide well.

6

People of Discernment

*The mature, . . . those whose faculties have been
trained by practice to distinguish good from evil.*
HEBREWS 5:14

If we think about discernment only at the critical junctures of our lives, we will remain immature, and at best we will stumble through to some kind of a decision. Ideally our lives should be ordered for discernment. We don't want just to practice discernment; we want to be discerning people. Those who practice discernment most effectively are those who over the years mature as discerners.

What does it mean to be a discerning person? Different components of a discerning life will be mentioned in this chapter, and the assumption is that without these components—all of them—we will approach the task of discernment either imbalanced or lame. It is not that without one of these we are incapable of making a wise choice; it is only that we are unnecessarily handicapped. Those who truly long to be discerning will seek to make each of the following part of the fabric of their daily experience. If these components are integrated into our spiritual experience, we will more likely be able to discern at particular decision points in our lives.

Prayer and Spiritual Receptivity

As I have already stressed, a discerning person is *an individual who prays*, who engages in personal communion with God. Prayer is often considered a time for petitioning God, and prayer does definitely include the component of intercession. But if prayer is to be the context for discernment, the prayer of communion is basic to being a discerning person. If we do not know how to fellowship with God in prayer, we will not know how to recognize and respond to the voice of God, the inner witness of the Spirit.

A discerning person is by definition a praying person. As Ernest Larkin puts it, "A solid, personal spirituality is the only consistent ground for distinguishing good and bad impulses, tendencies, aspirations, and decisions. Anything less is magical."[1] Nothing is so elemental to a personal spirituality and thus to becoming a discerner as learning how to pray and fostering an intimate relationship with God through prayer.

This means that we need to speak of *listening* prayer—prayer that is both speaking with God and attending to God, attentive to the still small voice of God, who speaks within the circumstances of our lives through the inner witness of the Spirit. A discerning person is characterized by what A. W. Tozer calls "spiritual receptivity."

Tozer's book *The Pursuit of God* has an unfortunate bias against the intellect and the imagination. But his discussion of "spiritual receptivity" is excellent. He notes that the critical difference between those who know communion with God and those who do not, those who "find" God and those who do not, is not a matter of "race, nationality, education, temperament, habit or personal qualities." Rather, he suggests that the difference is spiritual receptivity—a cultivated spiritual awareness, a lifelong habit of spiritual response. All people have some kind of inward longing for God. The difference is that these people, as Tozer puts it, "did something about it."[2]

Tozer acknowledges that behind this receptivity are the grace and prompting of God. But he suggests that this recognition of divine sovereignty must not paralyze us; rather, it should empower us toward an active response and a radical openness to God. The gift of God needs to be cultivated. The longing in our hearts, placed there by God, is either cultivated or suppressed and neglected. And this is most evident in our prayer.

Emotional Self-Understanding

Second, a discerning person *recognizes and understands his or her own emotional self.* Mixed-up emotions will only mean mixed-up signals. If our emotional experience is confused, we will not be able to find clarity as we seek to know what is best. Emotional upheaval will leave us confused about what we should be doing or what decision we should make.

In his book *Re-examining Conscience* John Carmody has some valuable insights regarding the need to be reflective and attentive to one's inner life, the emotional ups and downs of daily experience. The examination of conscience is much more than the traditional understanding of reviewing what sins one has committed. Rather, Carmody urges his readers to think of the examination of conscience as a careful reflection on what time has been doing to us in the recent past. He suggests we focus on the tender places—sadness and joy—which are important indicators of the life of the inner person. This assumes a basic honesty: not only a straightforward recognition of where we did well and where we blew it, but also a courageous acknowl-edgment of our emotional responses to what we have experienced, good or bad.

Carmody writes, "In starting to examine our consciences, we do well to fix our attention on the things that count, on the projects, persons and episodes that have left an emotional trace."[3] Such a careful and selective review of our recent past assumes something with respect to God: "God tends to move us, to want to teach us through our emotional gains and losses. He wants, as well, slowly to move us to some purchase on our emotions, some freedom from their dominance."[4]

Facing up to our joys and sorrows helps us come to grips with our responsibilities, and this turns us back to God in prayer. The examination of conscience, then, becomes part of an essential bridge between our activities in the world and our prayers.

The call to discernment is a call to a personal understanding of our emotional state: where we are angry, sad, discouraged, fearful, uncertain and disappointed. It is a call to face up to our inner aloneness and the darkness that we face at different points in our spiritual pilgrimage. The ideal response is honesty with ourselves and with God.

If we do not examine our lives and get in touch with our emotions, we will be controlled and blinded by our emotions—by fear, anger, discouragement and more. If we are not aware of our emotions, we cannot be discerning people. To be discerning we need to know ourselves. And this requires honesty. If we have had an extended pattern of not being honest with ourselves, it may take a long time to come to a sober realization of who we are and how we are responding to the events in our lives.

Humility and Self-Knowledge
Each of the characteristics of the discerning person listed so far

is important. But nothing is probably more crucial than this: a discerning person is an individual of humility. So in our quest to become discerning people, we need to understand both the nature of humility and what it means to experience it.

It is not a coincidence that in the *Spiritual Exercises* of Ignatius Loyola his words on humility immediately precede the explanation of the three times for making a choice or decision. John Wesley also emphasizes the importance of humility, seeming to echo Ignatius. For Wesley humility includes an awareness of sin and our need for repentance—a deep-rooted meekness before the mercy of God. But for Wesley humility is also evident in a personal disposition toward the purposes and will of God. This submission is the antithesis of self-exaltation and self-centeredness, and this state of humility is the only posture from which we can hear God.

Further, Wesley emphasizes that humility includes a healthy recognition that we are easily self-deceived. Knowing that we all live with a well-practiced ability for self-deception—for rationalizing misguided motives—should in itself keep us humble.

But we must go further. A person of humility will have another quality that is essential for discernment: *a true assessment and appreciation of their strengths, talents and abilities* as well as their limitations. As I have already suggested, the call of God and his direction will not violate who we are; on the contrary, it will reflect our strengths, abilities and even desires. This true measure of our selves is part of what it means to be humble.

St. Paul calls his readers to take a sober look at themselves (Rom 12:3) and respond to the call of God according to who they are. Some are leaders; some are not. Some are teachers; some are not. Humility means recognizing both our limitations and our potential, recognizing where we need others and where we can make a contribution to meeting the needs of others.

Humility graciously accepts both dimensions—our limitations and need for others and our potential, our ability to contribute to the well-being of others. The former does not diminish us; the latter does not inflate us. With sober judgment we simply accept who we are. And this humility is essential for effective discernment.

Therefore, part of becoming a discerning person is to grow in knowledge of one's self. St. Teresa of Ávila sees this as one of the most important characteristics of a mature, discerning person: "Knowing ourselves is something so important that I wouldn't want any relaxation ever in this regard, however high you may have climbed into the heavens. While we are on this earth nothing is more important to us than humility."[5]

Teresa makes this point while also affirming that we will never completely know ourselves if we do not strive to know God. For Teresa, and many spiritual masters who preceded her, self-knowledge is basic to and virtually synonymous with humility. Only in self-knowledge can we begin to sense the movement of God in our lives.

Self-knowledge includes self-acceptance—honestly owning who we are. If we do not accept who we are, and more, actually *like* who we are, we will probably not be able to meet God freely and respond to that encounter. We will always be attempting to be someone other than who we are; we will be living a lie. Thomas Merton is particularly insightful in this respect.[6] He suggests that only as I uncover what I really want, rather than what I think I want or should want, can I uncover who I really am. What I want is significant to God, Merton insists, because I am not made as a robot; I am not merely God's servant, but God's friend.

Actually, none of us can be all that we want to be. Growing self-knowledge helps us discover what our deepest desires are—what we really want, what is unique to us. This will help immeasurably in the discernment process, for few things block our ability to discern like the peremptory expectations and desires of others. To frustrate what *we* want is to frustrate God, for what we present to God as a living sacrifice (Rom 12:1-2) is something that we must be able to look upon with sober judgment (v. 3). We must, without apology, seek a greater understanding of our desires.

To resist this, Merton insists, is unconscious hypocrisy. We hypocritically assume that God's good and perfect will for us is something that we do not want to do, and that the more we dislike it, the more likely it is he will want us to do it! Ernest Larkin puts it well when he writes, "Basically *the* difficulty in all discernment is personal inauthenticity. If you are not in touch with yourself, if you don't know what is going on, you cannot hear the 'other,' even when the other is God."[7]

Merton suggests that we need to return to the simplicity of the child and discover the inner truth of who we are and what we long for. Honestly ask the question of yourself, *What do I want?* Then you can face separately the question, *What do others want and expect from me?* In so doing, of course, we must be prepared to take responsibility for our desires and accept the consequences of the choices we will make. But this is a small price to pay. In order to be free to see and respond to the best, we must begin by being honest about the desires of our hearts.

In this self-acceptance we experience a fundamental freedom. Tozer calls this a freedom from "pretense." Seeking to be or act like someone we are not is hypocrisy, Tozer notes. Sin is powerful in its deceit, particularly when because of sin we lie to ourselves and then fear that our real selves will be discovered. Tozer, like Merton, affirms that we need to return to a childlike simplicity, refusing to compare ourselves with others and graciously accepting ourselves.[8]

Self-Knowledge and Culture

Another part of self-knowledge is learning to *recognize how we have been shaped by our culture*. We are not usually alerted to our cultural identity until we have the opportunity to travel and experience another social context. But any encounter with individuals of another culture will to some degree show us that we are shaped by the social context in which we live.

I have the opportunity to visit Hong Kong rather frequently. It is the one country I visit where they drive on the left. When I come to cross a street in Hong Kong, though I know full well that they drive on the left, I still look left, not right, when I step off the curb. I have a deeply ingrained behavioral habit based on an assumption. And so I look left. I am still here to tell the story; I have yet to be hit by a Hong Kong bus. But I know that a few days or even several weeks in Hong Kong would not change my habit. Cultural conditioning goes deep.

The same applies to our values, our worldview, our sense of personal rights and our expectations. We are conditioned to expect certain comforts, privileges or rights. It could be that we are conditioned to ignore the needs of those less fortunate—the poor and the oppressed.

Our only hope is to begin a process of intentional reflection on our culture—the values that have shaped us, the norms and expectations that undergird the society in which we live. Reading about our society, examining our culture against the witness of Holy Scripture and reflecting on our behavior and attitudes together with others can all help the process.

Conscious of the Strategies of the Evil One

We need to be attentive to the voice of the Spirit; but whether we like it or not, there is a contrary voice that we must be alert to if we are to be discerning people. We need to be *conscious of and rigorously against the stratagem of the Evil One.* Just as we can be assured that the Lord is our Shepherd, who meets us as a friend and guides us as a heavenly Father, even so we can be certain of the desire of the Evil One to dissuade us from that which is good and perfect and best. Indeed, he succeeds if we consistently choose the second best.

The Evil One takes some standard approaches in his efforts to tempt us, play on our motives and weaknesses, and deter us from that which is best. Part of the genius of C. S. Lewis in his *Screwtape Letters,* however, is the recognition that the Enemy's approach is probably customized for each of us. A maturing discerner recognizes how the Evil One tends to work in his or her mind. There is a sense, of course, in which this is another dimension of self-knowledge.

Structures of Accountability

Another critical aspect of discernment is having structures of accountability, which include friends who know you well and hold you accountable. This is part of what it means to be in Christian community. We live in submission to one another in the community; further, we live in submission to those in authority over us within that community.

I need to emphasize again that we make our own decisions. We cannot expect others to either make our choices or take responsibility for our choices. We act for ourselves and do so in light of our own conscience. In this we stand alone. When the decisions we make are most pressing, when we are facing a choice that will profoundly affect us and those we love, we feel the aloneness of our humanity. And rightly so. We *are* alone.

But though we are alone in the actual decision, we need not be alone in the process of coming to that decision. We have the company of Christian believers—spiritual authority in our lives and friends who can help us understand the decision and are frank with us regarding the issues we face. Good decisions are made by those who know how to live with these two opposing poles—the solitariness of one's choice and the comfort of input from others along the way.

Rather than being independent and autonomous, effective discerners live in submission to constituted authority within the Christian community. Those who insist on getting their own way and who live in isolation (spiritual and emotional isolation, if not physical) are least likely to choose well. We were not created spiritual nomads; isolation violates our identity as human persons.

But more, we need the company of men and women whom we can call friends, individuals who refuse to flatter us and are quite prepared to call our bluff, question our motives, probe our fears and illusions, and call us to be true to ourselves and to God. They accept us, know us and want nothing for us but what is best. There are few if any greater treasures than this kind of friends, and the likelihood is that you will have very few. So nurture and cherish the friendships you have. And turn to these friends at the decision times of your life. Allow them to respond to your thoughts, be part of the process and encourage you in the tough choices you need to make. The decision you make is your own; but you do not need to be alone in the process of coming to that decision.

People Who Free Other People

In 1 Thessalonians 4:11 the apostle Paul urges us to make it our ambition to mind our own business. I have a hunch but am not able to prove empirically that discerning people free others to make their own choices—and "mind their own business." It is not that they do not care and are not willing to be generous and helpful. It is merely that they free others to discern for themselves.

Some feel they need to control others. They are happy to make other people's decisions for them. They feel they are God's gift to those around them, and they have an insatiable desire to "help." For some reason, though, when we fail to free others to choose well, we ourselves cannot choose well. When we poke our nose in other people's lives, our outward focus disables us and dulls the focus on our own decisions—a concentration we urgently need if we are to discern well. Those who have this problem usually do not see themselves as having a problem, and they do not realize that their focus on other people's actions, their inability to free others to act according to their own conscience, blinds them in their own decisions.

The implication is obvious. We need to continually allow others to respond to their own conscience. Running other people's lives undermines our ability to take charge of our own lives and respond fully and freely to the will of God. A helpful rule of thumb might be "Offer no unsolicited advice." It is a good way to keep you focused on your own pilgrimage rather than trying to live others' lives for them.

Routine and Order in Our Lives

Finally, one other characteristic of discerning people needs to be included in this list: their lives are marked by routine and order, a rhythm to life and work. Because each of us is a psychosomatic unity, if our lives are filled by disorder and high stress, we will likely become confused and bewildered internally. If our daily activity is not characterized by some measure of order, we will not be able to find the peace, the inner consolation, so necessary to discernment. To become discerning people we need to seek and find an order in our daily lives, a rhythm of prayer and service, work and leisure.

This list of qualities or characteristics of discerning people is really nothing more than a description of what it means to be a maturing and wise person. As we grow in faith and spiritual maturity, we will become discerning people, particularly if we recognize that at the heart of spirituality and wisdom is the desire to know, love and serve Christ.

The New Testament says very little about the procedure of discernment, but it says a great deal about the conditions that make discernment possible. Of primary importance is whether we are soil in which discernment can flourish. What is critical is that we nurture in our lives the conditions for effective discernment.

7

A Discernment Notebook

If any of you is lacking in wisdom, ask God,
who gives to all generously and
ungrudgingly, and it will be given you.
JAMES 1:5

Whathat follows are insights, perspectives and thoughts on different aspects of discernment. I have called this collection my notebook. These notes arise from the insights and comments made in response to questions of students or retreatants on the topic of discernment.

1. Other Perspectives on Discernment and Guidance

I have already identified two other outlooks on guidance or discernment that are commonly held among Christians, particularly evangelicals. The first might be called the *blueprint school;* the second could be described as the *wisdom school.*

Those of the blueprint school in effect believe that God has a perfect plan or blueprint for each person. This approach to understanding guidance concludes that there are three "wills" of God: his sovereign will for history; his moral will, in terms of good and evil; and his personal will for each individual. God has an ideal, detailed life plan uniquely designed for each person. Obviously, then, the goal of the Christian is simple: discover the will of God and follow this will. God has a plan for your life; all that is left is to find this plan and live by it. The assumption, of course, is that true happiness is found within God's will for your life. When it comes to marriage, vocation, the school you will attend, when you will go and when you will stay, you need to determine whether it is God's will or pattern for your life before you act.

We are to discover this will through a variety of means, often called "road signs," which we are to look for and take as directives. Circumstances, inner witness, wise counsel and often signs or "fleeces" (a reference to the experience of Gideon in Judges 6) all come together to help the believer know with certainty the will of God. Often those of this school speak of "doors." We look for open doors and expect God to close any doors we are not to follow or go through. Confidence or certainty that we are "in the Lord's will" comes through the particular coordination of the road signs—counsel, inner witness, circumstances, the one "open door."

But there are many problems with viewing divine guidance in this manner. First, there is the question of which kinds of decisions are to be made in this way and which are not. Does the blueprint apply to all decisions, including every minor decision of the day? If not, to what decisions does it apply? Does God never say, "It's up to you"? Does God have a perfect plan for each detail of our life? If so, we could spend all our time trying to figure out this plan rather than living!

Second, we need to consider how others are affected by what we sense to be the will of God for our lives. We may think God's plan for us is one thing, but what if another person affected by that "will of God" does not agree? What happens when God directs me to marry someone who then responds by marrying someone else? Or what happens when I think God is telling me to attend a particular university but I am denied admission?

The blueprint view does not take sufficient account of the whole variety of variables that make up our lives. The biggest variable may well be our own failures. If we make a mistake and fail to find the plan of God for our life, or if we follow it but someone else fails to perform as we think they should in accordance with this revealed plan, where does that leave us? Out of the will of God?

Finally, what concerns me most about this perspective is the implicit view of God. Is God a determiner of our lives? Do we really have sufficient biblical evidence to conclude that God has a plan for each life—a plan that is predetermined? God seems to be much more dynamic in his relationship with his children. The blueprint approach seems to focus primarily on the will of God rather than on God himself. Christians are often left trying various techniques and methods to find this will, and these methods often come dangerously close to a kind of superstitious divination.

The wisdom school really arose in response to the blueprint perspective and is ably presented by Gary Friesen in his book *Decision Making and the Will of God,* which includes a forceful critique of the blueprint school. Friesen argues that God gives us his moral will and grants us principles (wisdom) by which we are to live. We must then live and act according to these principles. We make our choices on the basis of biblical principles, particularly the command to love God and neighbor. As we grow in wisdom, we apply this godly sense to our earthly situations. Friesen rejects any implication that we are like chess pieces on a chessboard and that God merely moves us around. He suggests rather that we mature in faith and God gives us real wisdom with which to act. From this perspective, the prayer for wisdom in James 1 is wisdom to make a decision, not a prayer to uncover a prepackaged divine choice.[1]

Thus according to Friesen and others we cannot say "God told me to do it" as a justification for questionable actions. The blueprint model, Friesen suggests, leaves people handcuffed, waiting for the signs to determine their course of action. Instead we should appreciate that God is "leaving it up to [us]," and we are to act in our own judgment. God has given us the wisdom to act. When we are left passively waiting for something more direct from God, Friesen asserts, the blueprint teaching is unhelpful and discouraging. Further, he believes that the blueprint model denies the validity of personal preferences when there are equally good options. Finally, he says, the blueprint approach undermines the clear expectation of Scripture that mature reflection and wise consideration will be a part of the normal Christian experience.

While I am sympathetic in many ways to the wisdom approach to guidance and grant that we have much to learn from this perspective about what it means to grow in wisdom and exercise wisdom with sanctified minds before God, certain questions must be asked. I have reservations about the conclusions of the wisdom school. First, I doubt that God is so removed from our life situations. The wisdom approach has been called a practical deism: God sets us on our way, gives us a Bible by which to live and then wishes us bon voyage, leaving us on our own. Klaus Bockmuehl has made an apt observation: as Christians we must deny the principle of self-rule, even when that rule is carried out in accordance with Scripture. Christ himself clearly lived by the Spirit in submission to the Father—a relationship that was intimate and dynamic.[2]

Another concern I have is that the wisdom model takes little if any account of our emotions, which have a powerful effect on how we think and can easily shape and potentially distort the decision-making process. Further, the wisdom model fails to adequately deal with the reality of mixed motives that inevitably shape the process of making a choice. We need a model for decisions and discernment that enables us to come to terms with our emotional makeup as well as the motives, confused or otherwise, that influence our thoughts.

Friesen rightly rejects the blueprint model, but then loses touch with the classic mystical tradition. Friesen's book is valuable in its affirmation of the way of wisdom (we are adult children of God). But he fails to draw on our spiritual heritage. He calls the blueprint model the traditional model, but actually the view he critiques is *recent* in historical terms. "Tradition" takes us back to a far more ancient perspective, one that I have sought to articulate in this study.

2. The Use of Fleeces and Signs

Many sincere Christians, particularly those of what I have called the blueprint school, see the experience of Gideon and his fleeces as a pattern appropriate for Christians today. Gideon, when called of God, sought to confirm this call by placing a sheepskin on the ground overnight. In the morning, if the fleece remained dry while the ground was wet with dew, this would, in Gideon's mind, verify the call of God. But though he received this confirmation, he then went further. The next night he again put out the fleece and waited to see if this time it was wet while the ground was dry. It was. And he saw this as double confirmation of God's call. (The story is found in Judges 6.)

Some contemporary Christians have used signs or "fleeces" as means of confirming the will of God or determining this will.

But we may appropriately question whether this is a valid approach to knowing the purposes of God. Is Gideon an example we should follow? While many, no doubt, can tell stories indicating that God gave his blessing to this approach, certain concerns need to be raised.

First, the Bible explicitly forbids divination, and the fleece approach to signs comes dangerously close to a magical use of time and things. Gary Friesen puts it well when he writes, "Hunches, whatever I think after I pray, promise boxes, dropping the Bible and pointing [your] finger, are quasi forms of . . . divination."[3]

Second, requests for signs or fleeces force the hand of God. God does use signs. Mary the mother of the Lord was given a sign to confirm the word of God. But God chose the sign and the time when the sign would be revealed. The use of a fleece assumes that we have the right to determine the sign and when God is to reveal his will.

God must have the initiative. We are not free to determine the context in which God will speak and guide; we cannot coerce him. God, to be God, must be Lord of the situation and of our discernment. In the true task of discernment, we cannot determine for God how and when he will confirm his purposes for us.

Third, I wonder whether we can justify this approach when we are indwelt by the Spirit of God. Even if the validity of signs or fleeces can be shown, these methods do not seem consonant with our friendship with God. Not only is the use of a fleece impersonal, but it almost sounds like a childish game that we are playing with God.

We have no reason to believe that Gideon was right in setting out the fleece. The Bible merely describes his actions. We could just as easily conclude that he was testing God, which is condemned by Scripture. But apart from Gideon, for Spirit-filled believers who live following Pentecost surely this approach to divine guidance is inappropriate. Our basis of communion with God is not signs but his indwelling presence. Our fellowship with God does not need to be mediated through quasi-magical activities, for we have the opportunity and privilege of friendship with God.

3. The Use (and Abuse) of the Bible

The Bible is the written Word of God, and the Bible is used by many Christians as a tool to make a decision or determine God's word for them. While God certainly intends to guide his people through Holy Scripture, it is important that we use the Bible correctly, according to both the nature and the purpose of Scripture.

Some Christians use the Bible as a kind of sign book, seeking some verse or phrase that will become their verse or promise or insight for a time of decision. By chance, it seems, their eyes come across a verse that gives the impression of speaking directly to their situation, and they use this as confirmation of the direction they should go or the decision they should make. In so doing they come dangerously close to abusing rather than using the Bible. The Bible is not a sign book. Further, this approach hints of divination and a kind of magical use of the Bible.

While we must acknowledge that God has provided some very specific and detailed guidance through the Bible, this is not normative. It is not something to be sought. If the Spirit guides us in some specific action through the prompting of a verse or passage of Scripture, that is fine. But to seek this guidance could easily lead us astray. We will force Scripture to say things it does not say. We will grant undue weight to the choices we make, attributing them to God's Word when they came merely from our own impressions that arose in reading the Scriptures. God has led in this way, but it is not something to be sought.

The Bible, used correctly, is read as letters, Gospels, narratives and other literary forms written by individuals in different cultures and contexts under inspiration of the Holy Spirit. Many of these documents were addressed to specific people in specific settings. The letters of St. Paul to the Corinthians were written to the church in Corinth. For us to understand God's Word for us today, we seek the principles and norms that lie within the specific words of Paul to the Corinthians and apply them to our contemporary situation. Thus we cannot consider every word or statement in the Bible as somehow written personally to us.

Not every promise in the Bible is for us. Some biblical promises were for a specific people or person at a particular time. Abraham and Abraham alone, for example, received the promise that his descendants would be like the sand of the seashore. David, as king of Israel, received a promise that his descendant would also rule as king over Israel. We abuse Scripture when we disregard the original historical context in which it was first written and apply it uncritically to our situations.

The purpose of Scripture must also be kept in mind: to enable us to know and understand the truth and grow in faith and wisdom. The Bible gives us principles by which we come to decisions. In many respects the Bible gives boundaries within which Christians can make decisions; and for this reason a discerning Christian is one who is profoundly influenced by Scripture. But we violate Scripture when we use it for the specifics of discernment, when we are choosing between two options that are not addressed in Scripture. Given those two options, God may lead one believer one way and another believer the other. The Bible gives no specific insight, and to seek that insight is unnecessary and unhelpful.

4. What About Open Doors?

Some Christians believe that discernment is not necessary because the wisdom and purposes of God can be determined through what are called "open doors." Those who teach this approach to decision-making believe that if a door is closed—that is, if an opportunity is denied—it is not God's will. On the other hand, if a door is open—if the opportunity is there and available—then this is a declaration of God's will. Often it is said that if one door is closed, another will be opened.

But life is not that simple, and discernment is not that easy. First, this understanding leaves unresolved the problem of the Christian who is confronted with two open doors, two options that based on all considerations are equally valid. Christians who have no other frame of reference but the open door are at a loss how to proceed.

Second, there is another question to be asked: is a closed door necessarily an indication that this is not the direction we should go? The people of Israel faced a closed door, you might say, when they crossed the Jordan River and came upon the impressive walled city of Jericho. In the case of this closed door, God's word was not "Turn and go another way"; it was, rather, "Walk around the city seven times!" A closed door does not nullify the need for discernment; we must still determine the wisdom and purposes of God. The fact of a closed door is just that, a fact. It means nothing in itself. It is not a substitute for discernment.

Third, an open door is not a sure indication that we are to go in that particular direction. Consider what St. Paul wrote of a predicament he faced in Troas: "When I came to Troas to proclaim the good news of Christ, a door was opened for me in the Lord; but my mind could not rest because I did not find my brother Titus there. So I said farewell to them and went on to Macedonia" (2 Cor 2:12-13). A door was opened to Paul, but he did not have peace, he tells his readers; his mind could not rest. The open door did not mean that discernment was not necessary.

Whether doors are closed or open, it would seem, is only one consideration in the process of coming to a decision. It cannot even be the primary factor. There may be two open doors. There may be closed doors that need to be "walked around," or there may be open doors but no peace in our mind.

An opportunity or an open door is surely a significant factor in our discernment. We may be offered a job; a group may wish to nominate us for a position of leadership; a marriage proposal may come. The opportunity may be there; the door may be open. But discernment is still necessary. Is this opportunity the best for us at this time in terms of the glory of God? Is this the direction we should go? Being nominated does not mean we must accept the nomination. Discernment is still necessary. Being offered a job does not mean we must accept. It could be that God would have us stay with our current position. We still need to ask: what is God's best?

5. One Step at a Time

A basic principle of spiritual discernment and guidance is that we are seeking the best for today, for this time and place, for this point in our pilgrimage. God leads us one step at a time. We may wish that God would map out the next few years or even our whole life for us. Some Christians are stymied in decision-making because they demand that all their questions be answered, with all the implications of a decision clearly delineated. They may feel uneasy making a commitment to a new position because they do not know all that will be entailed in accepting that role.

But this long-term knowledge is not granted to us. We cannot see beyond the immediate future. God leads us one step at a time, and we accept this as part of what it means to be his children. We are discerning only for today, not for the whole of our life. Often we make discernment more difficult than it is by trying to answer all the questions, identify all the potential problems and make every piece fit comfortably into the puzzle.

I also find it helpful to remember that God may well lead us to one point in order that we may, from there, see where he calls us to go—a place or a role we cannot see now. We may not be able to see all that he has for us; but we do not need to. We need to see only the next step into which he calls us.

6. Promises to Keep

The conditional nature of spiritual discernment requires that we be careful in our promises or even our statements of intent. I remember, shortly after I arrived in the Philippines, hearing another new missionary state in a public gathering that he had been called to the Philippines for life and would be there until he retired. As he spoke, I could see former missionaries to Vietnam at the back of the room, and I could not help but wonder what they were thinking. They may have gone to Vietnam for life, but they were forced to leave in 1975. The young missionary who spoke certainly had noble intentions, but they were naive. All we know is what we can do now and for today.

For most decisions, we can only make commitments in the light we have today. There are exceptions to this. In marriage, for example, we make a commitment "till death do us part." We can also make a vow of celibacy and determine that it will be a call for life. But most of our choices and decisions must be made with an understanding that we make this choice or decision within the light we have today. Tomorrow our circumstances may change.

It could be, for example, that the Lord would lead a person

to the Philippines today but in time lead her elsewhere. Do we not close down the door to the wisdom and counsel of God when we overstate the significance of his direction today? God is not capricious. He will not send you to the Philippines today and to Africa tomorrow. Of course not. But we must not bind God or ourselves by overstating the significance of the guidance we receive today. We must therefore avoid promises and commitments that undermine our ability to respond to the voice of God in the future.

7. Competition with Others

In *Becoming Christian, Becoming Adult* James Fowler makes a significant affirmation when he notes that as Christian believers, assured together that we are each called of God, we never need to compete with another person for a position or an opportunity.[4] A biblical view of vocation rejects the idea that we need to "get ahead" in life, which by implication means that we need to get ahead of others. God is big enough for all of us, and if in the providence of God another person is chosen for a position we were interested in, this is good, and God has not forsaken anyone.

Within the kingdom purposes of God we do not need to be grabbing after positions or worried that if someone else gets an opportunity our career development will be stunted. We can freely accept and actually delight in the opportunities that others receive, recognizing that God in his grace, wisdom and mercy calls and provides for all. We can and must discern God's purposes for us without competing with others.

8. The Place of Fasting

The purpose of fasting is to encourage discernment. Fasting is spoken of in some Christian groups as something that accompanies prayer when we are very serious about our prayer. The notion seems to be that when we are most committed to prayer and intercession, we will fast, and that our fasting reveals the seriousness with which we take prayer in general and our current requests in particular. But in so doing we come dangerously close to testing God.

Fasting is not a means of persuading God to take us more seriously and hear our prayers. Rather, it is a means, if anything, to enable *us* to hear God. For some reason, when our stomachs are empty our minds are keener, our hearts more sensitive, more open and thus more discerning. We are more alert spiritually. We fast not that God would hear us, but that we would be able to hear God.

Fasting, then, is an appropriate spiritual discipline. Some have found it valuable to fast weekly, perhaps from lunch one day through lunch the next day, on a set day each week. Others have found it valuable to have an extended period of fasting as a means to come clean before God and attend to his voice—perhaps every few weeks or months, or once a year. It is best to see fasting as a discipline that has helped many Christians deepen their spiritual walk and discern God's voice. It is not a requirement for discernment, but it is a discipline that maturing Christians have often chosen to practice.

9. A Bias Against Change

Terry Muck, in an editorial reflecting on the process of change and the decision to take a new job, gives a single piece of advice that is worth remembering: Create a bias against change. He notes:

> We are fickle creatures. . . . The grass-is-greener syndrome is a powerful pull, and too many things conspire to make us think we can do better elsewhere.

Our transitory society makes a virtue out of short job tenures and temporary experiences.

The Christian concept of faithfulness endorses a willingness to stick things out even when the going gets tough.[5]

We cannot be running off for a day of discernment every time a new opportunity arises or a new door opens. Muck is right. We need to develop perseverance. We need to reject the fickleness of our society and the temptation to run from a situation every time the going is difficult. It would perhaps be valid to say that unless we have clear evidence that we should leave, we should stay. The bias should be against change.

10. The Value of a Journal

Many Christians have found great value in keeping a spiritual journal as an instrument by which they monitor their pilgrimage with God and respond to the temptations, difficulties and circumstances of their lives. The primary value of a journal is self-knowledge. It is a place to record our feelings, frustrations, impressions and reactions to our world and to developments that are important to us. It is a place to note our joys and sorrows.

But a journal is probably most valuable when we describe the transition times of our lives—the process of coming to decisions, the times of discernment and the final choices that we eventually make. As a record of our interaction with the Spirit, a journal becomes an invaluable resource for knowing who we are and how we are, maturing or growing in our faith and our relationship with the Spirit.

It should go without saying that we write for ourselves alone. There is an audience of only one. As soon as we think that others may read our notes or as soon as we consider writing for publication, we defeat our purpose. We may draw on a journal when we write a memoir, but the journal in itself must be private.

11. Husbands and Wives

As a general rule act only when you agree with your spouse. The two of you need to have a similar level of peace regarding the choice or decision. My wife and I believe that God will lead us together. Sometimes, of course, one of us may know the direction of God first. But if so, that one waits for the other. We do not act in such a manner that we violate each other's ability to discern and know the peace of God.

I have found this to be tremendously liberating. It frees me to seek the peace of God in the knowledge that my peace will be confirmed or questioned by how the Lord is speaking to my wife. Probably because we have different temperaments, she usually has a sense of God's purposes earlier than I do. She seems to have a keener sensitivity. It takes me longer to slow down, still the mind and attend to the promptings of the Spirit. But she waits for me and sees my process of discernment as confirming the sense she has in her mind.

My wife and I are "one flesh" in the mind of God; I can only assume that God, then, will guide us as one. Further, both my wife and I are filled with the Spirit and capable of responding to the prompting of the Spirit. I can easily assume that God speaks to her as readily as he does to me. God leads us together.

12. The Conditional Nature of Discernment

I have already stressed that discernment is profoundly personal. I affirm the priority of the individual conscience. St. Paul insists in Romans 14 that all of us must respond in faith to our own conscience and not presume that our neighbor will respond in the same manner. Even on a matter like violence, we cannot say that physical force is always wrong at all times. Jesus himself responded with violence to the money changers in the temple and then responded passively when he was arrested in Gethsemane. So we cannot judge our neighbor. God may lead two persons in remarkably similar circumstances to respond in very different ways. Discernment is personal.

But we need to go further. Basic Christian humility demands that even when we believe we have the mind of the Lord, we hold our conviction lightly. There are few things as wearisome as the fanatic who has no self-doubts. Wise people are confident and prepared to act courageously, but they are also humble enough to remember that they can be wrong. We would do well, then, to discern conditionally, recognizing our potential for self-delusion and the possibility that others may see a situation quite differently.

13. Dreams

Carl Jung is notable in part for his unique insight into the nature and potential significance of dreams. Many students of the spiritual life have sought to incorporate his insights into a Christian understanding of discernment. Their conclusions are noteworthy: that dreams are significant in the spiritual life and attention to our dreams can assist us in examining our own subconscious.

I find the perspective of Ronald Barnes helpful on the place of dreams in discernment.[6] He recognizes that the analysis of dream content can be a major source of distraction if we become preoccupied with it. Barnes concludes that understanding dreams can be very helpful in the quest for self-knowledge but that this is, at most, an auxiliary means of spiritual growth and thus of discernment.

14. Authority and Organizational Decisions

At different points in the history of the church there have been different perspectives on the nature and significance of spiritual authority within the Christian community. While many Christians have no structure of spiritual accountability, others fall prey to another spiritually confused perspective. They absolve themselves of responsibility and see the heart of their spirituality to be submitting to spiritual authority. Sometimes this is the perceived authority of a spouse or of a pastor. At other times within the church, or within mission or ministry organizations, there is an unquestioned submission to directors or supervisors.

But submission within the Christian community never overrides the need for discernment and personal responsibility for our decisions. The organization can never replace conscience. No one, not even our superior, can discern for us. We do need to submit, but our submission cannot violate our own conscience. True maturity means that we make our decisions and take responsibility for them. We abdicate responsibility for our lives when, with pious sentimentalism, we claim that we are only submitting to the authority of others, letting others make our decisions for us as though we were children.

We cannot live in peace and humility unless we submit to spiritual authority and learn to live in humble submission as the pattern of our lives. But this submission is qualified. We do not violate our own conscience. But more, we are not absolved of personal responsibility for our life and our actions. We can live and work as self-directed men and women, seeking the mind of God, while also living in submission to constituted authority, whether in the church or in our spheres of work and responsibility in the world.

15. Learning from Past Decisions

We can gain some of the best insights into ourselves—our character, the patterns of our thoughts and behavior—by looking at the decisions we have made in the past. A helpful exercise is to look at a significant decision and reflect on it thoroughly. Past choices can help us make better choices the next time around. We see patterns of behavior and thought that reflected a weakness in our character. We can detect unhealthy patterns and watch for them and avoid them as we face decisions today.

Members of a clearness committee might ask about past choices, especially if they are similar in kind to the one faced today. For example, if you are considering resigning from an organization, they might ask you, as you ask yourself, whether you are handling this situation in the very same way you handled a previous crisis or conflict. Perhaps there is a negative pattern of behavior to which you need to be alerted.

Now I need to stress that we must avoid second-guessing ourselves and our past decisions. We have made those choices; the past is behind us. There is no value in reliving poor decisions and castigating ourselves for our foolishness. Rather, we review the past as an exercise of learning and self-knowledge.

By looking at our decisions, we learn about ourselves and about decision-making. And, naturally, we become more accomplished in the art of discernment. We probably learn as much from our failures and mistakes as from the times in which we chose well. This comes in part from learning to recognize our capacity for self-deception on the one hand and from becoming more attentive to the voice of God on the other.

16. The Need to Frame a Decision Well

Often when we cannot come to resolution in a decision-making process or seemingly can get no clarity through discernment, the problem is that we have not framed our question well. We have not formulated the problem or question in a way that truly clarifies our options and enables us to hear God.

First, as already noted, we need to be sure that we are seeking to discern between two "goods," not between good and evil.

Second, it should also be clear that they are two truly equal alternatives. That is, we discern between marriage and celibacy, not between celibacy and marriage to a particular person. We first need to resolve an openness to marriage before we consider to whom we might become married.

Third, we should be certain that we are genuinely open to all legitimate alternatives. We may frame a question and seek to discern the Lord's mind on a matter, choosing between A and B. But we cannot hear the Lord because God is drawing our attention to C.

And fourth, sometimes we are attempting to make too many decisions at the same time, and in the interplay of decisions we are confused and bewildered in our attempt to hear the Lord. When this happens, we need to clarify our basic decision, or the most urgent or immediate decision about which we will pray and discern.

8

Blocks to
Discernment

*For this very reason, you must make every effort to support your
faith with goodness, and goodness with knowledge,
and knowledge with self-control, and self-control with endurance,
and endurance with godliness, and godliness
with mutual affection, and mutual affection with love.
For if these things are yours and are increasing among you,
they keep you from being ineffective and unfruitful
in the knowledge of our Lord Jesus Christ.*
2 PETER 1:5-8

God *is sovereign. He is not obligated to respond to us when we*
seek his face. True faith recognizes this and allows God to be
God—free to respond according to his wisdom. Patience with
God, and particularly with the timing of God, is essential for
spiritual maturity. Sometimes, then, in the discernment process,
we cannot seem to find a solution or get a sense of direction and
peace. The answer at these times is simply that we need to wait.
We need to be patient with God. This will be discussed more in
a chapter that follows.

But as often as not, the block to discernment is not the timing
of God but obstacles in our own minds that bungle up the process
of discernment. We can be our own worst enemy when it comes
to making a good choice. Freedom for discernment comes

through growing self-knowledge that includes the recognition that we each have mental blocks that inhibit us. Sometimes they are misconceptions; at other times they are prejudices or unresolved personal problems. Whatever the internal factor, we cannot discern well until the obstacle is acknowledged and resolved.

In a sense there is always a block to discernment that we need to overcome in order to apprehend the voice of God. Openly identifying some of these hindrances may help us make a remedial diagnosis. Each decision is an occasion to grow in deeper self-knowledge, each choice a time in which we come to greater resolution of our identity and character.

But sometimes certain obstacles consistently obstruct us, effectively disabling us time after time when we seek the mind and purposes of God. I will begin by identifying blocks that are more obvious; afterward I will discuss those that are more subtle, more difficult to detect and potentially more controversial. What follows is of greatest value if we are honest with ourselves.

Physical Blocks

The two physical obstacles to discernment, other than sickness itself, are *fatigue due to overextension* and *sloth due to inactivity.* Margaret Goldsbury calls fatigue from overextension a "misguided generosity."[1] Men and women, in their eagerness to serve Christ and do good, often take on more than they can do and neglect necessary times of leisure and rest. Others are sluggish from the lack of a good diet and regular exercise. Either imbalance creates mental and spiritual slothfulness.

I have had the disheartening experience of watching a friend in the throes of an important decision process, knowing full well that he was too tired to decide well, so exhausted from overwork and stress that he could not effectively discern the mind of the Lord. Such extreme weariness is a sign of desolation. It is unwise and presumptuous to attempt a decision at times like this. We do well to begin by finding extended time for rest, for sleep if necessary. It would probably be good to get some distance, if possible, from our responsibilities. When we are physically over-extended, we cannot discern well.

I said above that sickness is a physical obstacle to discernment. But it is worth noting that this is probably more the case with severe or traumatic illness. In other cases many Christians have found that through sickness they have been particularly conscious of the work of the Spirit in their hearts and minds. In a time of extended recuperation or recovery, believers may hear God speak in a way that could hardly have happened in the hectic or ordinary routine of life. One wonders whether at times the Lord allows sickness simply because that is the only way he can get our attention.

We pray better when we are rested. We are embodied souls. We are physical beings, and therefore how we are feeling physically invariably affects our capacity to hear God.

Psychological and Emotional Blocks

There are several psychological blocks that impede discernment. Goldsbury suggests that a lack of imagination is one psychological barrier to discernment.[2] Sometimes we cannot recognize the direction of God for the simple reason that we are not open to the possibility. It is not that we are unwilling; it is more that the possibility never crossed our minds, and so we did not recognize the call or direction of God. Sometimes our perspective on life and on our individual potential is limited by the scope of our imagination.

As a spiritual mentor, I often find that sometimes women are unable to recognize the call of God in part because of preconceived notions of what women cannot or should not do within the church. I frequently need to ask them: "Apart from the limitations imposed on women by the church, could it be that God is calling you to this ministry?" At other times individuals have a low self-image that limits their ability to recognize a wonderful opportunity that represents God's call. An automatic "I could never be that or do that" undercuts the process of discernment.

This is often evident when people face retirement. Some seem to give up on life; others see a whole range of options and opportunities. The difference often involves just having an imagination—seeing what there might be that God would have for me after this life transition.

Another psychological block to discernment is fear, which can rear its ugly head in a variety of forms. Some are afraid of failure and so are not prepared to respond to the call of God or even be open to it. Others are afraid not so much of failure as of what others will say. This "fear of men" is a powerful force in undermining the ability of men and women to hear and respond to the voice of God.

Related to this is our awareness of the expectations of others, which can be like a straitjacket to our discernment. I believe that the fear of what others will say or think, combined with the expectations of others, is the single most powerful block to effective discernment within the Christian community. Fear of others, combined with a sense of obligation to fulfill others' expectations, is always crippling.

We do need to be sensitive to the expectations of the community. We are called to love one another; we are to live in mutual submission. Thus the expectations and desires of others are a factor in our decision-making, and should be. But when the expectations of others become the primary consideration, it is a block to effective discernment. Some are unable to respond as adult children of God to the prompting and directives of God because their strong-minded, strong-willed parents have not freed them to respond and hear God's voice. Many parents have designs on their children's futures that in effect undermine their daughter's or son's ability to respond freely to God.

That is but the beginning. Pastors are often crippled by the expectations of their congregations. They easily get caught in the trap of trying to please all their parishioners, or at least the most demanding. But if, as pastors, we are servants of all, we are probably servants of none. We are just running back and forth trying to keep people happy. If we are men and women of conscience and principle, we will have to live with failing to meet others' expectations. Effective ministry will simply require that we disappoint some. Accepting this can free us to respond to the voice and expectations of God.

But there is another kind of fear that can serve as a powerful block in the process of discernment: the fear that arises from previous difficulty and troublesome experiences. Perhaps a woman was abused by men in her childhood and now finds it difficult to trust herself to a man in marriage. Perhaps a pastor had a difficult seminary experience or was mistreated in an early pastorate and now, years later, has difficulty hearing God's call back into parish ministry. Merely recognizing the source of our pain and fear can be a big step toward recognizing that our discernment is affected by these experiences.

Another psychological block is that of the perfectionist, the fastidious individual who has a horror of making a mistake. This crippling insistence on getting things right in every way before stepping out, of insisting on seeing how every detail will look before acting, keeps people from knowing the freedom found in discernment, a freedom that always includes elements of the unknown. Actually the perfectionist's problem is a fear of failure.

For this fear, as for each fear described above, there is a solution. To discern effectively, we need to begin by acknowledging our fears before God. Then we can simply ask God to carry those anxieties for us. Only then can we know the peace, the consolation, that is essential for discernment (Phil 4:6-7). I find it particularly helpful to take time during a day or period of prayer to enumerate my fears, to list them and then intentionally ask the Father to carry them. Only then can I receive the peace, the inner serenity, from which I can discern well and make a good decision.

For any number of reasons, people can get caught in a pattern of vacillation or procrastination. Their failure to choose and follow through on a decision has nothing to do with the guidance of God. Some impulsive fear is keeping them from the choice they are called to make. Naming this block is the first step to resolving and removing the obstacle from one's mind.

On the other hand, some are precipitous or make premature decisions, often as an attempt to relieve stress. High levels of stress interfere with our capacity to think well, consider our alternatives, review the potential consequences and attend in peace to the voice of God. Those living under high stress are well advised to watch for the propensity to make premature judgments and rash decisions.

Yet another psychological or emotional block is anger. Anger and an unforgiving spirit will always block discernment. Anger itself is not a sin. It could well be a true and right response to a wrong committed against you or someone you love. But anger, of its very nature, limits our ability to hear and respond to God. And so the apostle urges us not to let the sun go down on our anger (Eph 4:26). We are not to sleep with unresolved tension or anger. We are to move on, forgive and allow the Lord himself to restore our inner peace.

The danger of unresolved anger is that it burns deep within our psyche. It undercuts our joy, hardens our heart and dulls our mind. Angry men and women cannot be discerning individuals, in part because anger blinds us, makes us narrow-minded and leaves our heart insensitive to the voice of God.

If we want to be discerning people, we need to cultivate the spiritual habit of resolving anger. It is best, in the words of my father, to "keep short accounts with God." The longer anger is allowed to settle in our hearts and become deep-seated brooding and bitterness, the more difficult it will be for us to come to resolution and peace. Anger has the capacity to scorch our souls and blind us to the prompting of the Spirit. The sooner we move on from our anger, forgive the wrongdoer and accept God's peace, the better.

Another emotional block to discernment is unacknowledged mourning. Mourning is any inner pain and sorrow due to loss. The death of someone who is loved or appreciated will lead to mourning. But we need to also consider any loss of opportunity or the loss of a home or item that was special to us. There is also the pain of separation, when our children leave home or when we move to another city and feel the emptiness that comes with leaving our friends. If the pain of this loss or separation is ignored or denied, our hearts carry the weight and in effect remain broken and burdened. And we remain in desolation, sometimes unconsciously.

Many of us believe mistakenly that we should not cry at times of pain or freely acknowledge the sorrow in our hearts at death. Such a notion is not Christian. Jesus himself freely wept at the death of Lazarus, even though he knew that in a matter of moments Lazarus would live. Death was still death. Only as we acknowledge our pain and actually feel it can we begin to know healing. Only as we mourn can our mourning be turned to joy.

Finally, cynicism is another emotional block to discernment. Cynicism can be thought of as unresolved discouragement. Like anger and mourning, discouragement is not a sin. It is a natural reaction to living in a broken world. Any person who longs and works for God and seeks to do the will of God in this world will become discouraged. There will be setbacks; people will let us down. We will fail. But if discouragement is allowed to settle into our hearts, we become cynical. In discouragement we can either respond to the encouragement that God offers, through his Word or through others who bring encouragement, or allow cynicism to grow in our hearts. And the cynic cannot discern effectively. Before we can decide well, we need to know some measure of hope; we need to acknowledge our discouragement and receive the encouragement of God.

It is unwise to neglect our emotions or fail to take seriously the possibility that our inner turmoil might undermine our capacity to discern and decide well. Emotions have an impact on both the final decision made and the process by which we come to the decision. Emotional upheaval distorts our ability to think clearly, listen clearly and respond with clarity and courage.

Theological Blocks

There are various theological factors that block effective discernment. These pertain to the area of belief and understanding. One example is our view of God. If we think of God as a severe, unloving judge, we will expect God to act in a demanding and implacable way. Some view God as a grand chess player who moves people around to suit his purposes. I am increasingly convinced that this pragmatist view of God is not true to God's self-revelation in Scripture. Though it is true that God calls us to himself so that we may be a blessing to others, this ministry to others is itself essential to our well-being and joy. Our vocation is always true to who we are. The desires of our hearts are important to God; he implants them in our hearts.

Our view of God directly affects our ability to discern the word of God to us, and therefore we need to nurture our understanding of God as the Father of our Lord Jesus Christ, as the Good Shepherd who cares for his sheep.

Our view of vocation can also be a significant factor in discernment. Some, for example, see the missionary or apostolic vocation as inherently more sacred than other vocations and therefore superior. A nonreligious vocation, as a teacher, artist, lawyer or businessperson, is viewed as less than holy. This false notion of vocation, this failure to recognize that all vocations are potentially sacred, has led sincere Christians to respond to Christ by almost automatically choosing the "highest" calling rather than listening for and accepting the call of God for them as individuals.

Another perspective on vocation is a fruit of the Western emphasis on the useful and productive, which is often the basis for determining the worth of a vocation or occupation. It is difficult to recognize and respond to the call of God to be an artist in the current social and cultural climate. A theological misconception essentially blocks the ability of individuals to see, recognize and respond to God's call.

It is my impression that artists, in particular, struggle with the pragmatism that judges an individual's worth in terms of what is useful or immediately practical. Those who are called to be musicians, especially classical musicians, or artists or playwrights tend to be affirmed only if their work is immediately pleasing to us or seemingly has immediate benefits for the life and witness of the church. But the call of the artist needs to be nurtured for the long-term well-being of the church. It is only shortsightedness that leads us to denigrate this invaluable vocation.

Another potential theological block is our understanding of the love and forgiveness of God. If we have sinned, our guilt will impede us; we must confess, repent and come clean before God. But for many, the fact of their sin remains in their consciousness. They then continue to strive to atone for their wrongdoing. Rather than freely accepting the forgiveness of God, they are, in subtle and sometimes less-than-subtle ways, seeking to pay for their sins. They work harder and longer and with more determination than others because of a vague inner sense that they are not worthy. In discernment they will often lean toward what appears to be a more difficult alternative. To discern well, we need to know the freedom of God's forgiveness.

We also can become theologically confused about the will of God, usually because of preconceptions about what God requires of us. The Quakers used to follow a general rule that the option involving difficulty, suffering and sacrifice was more than likely the true way. The way of comfort, or the alternative that was more attractive, was the route to be avoided. Obviously this in effect predetermines God's will by a theological quirk. But contemporary evangelical Protestants seem to make the opposite assumption. If there are two job offers, they are inclined to take the one that pays best and has the most benefits. We have the opposite predilection, a theological bias that, just as surely as with the Quakers, undermines our ability to recognize and respond to the voice of God.

This is but a sampling of the kinds of factors that can undermine our ability to be effective in discernment. Part of self-knowledge is recognizing what factors, predilections, biases, internal emotional factors and perceptions could undermine our ability to be discerning. Effective discernment includes honest self-evaluation as we seriously consider what factors may be crippling our ability to know the mind of God. Sometimes the block to our discernment may be a passing or temporary problem that needs resolution. But most of us have inclinations or blocks to discernment that reflect theological biases or emotional crutches to which we frequently return.

During discernment we need to acknowledge our inclinations and recognize how they will shape our prayers and our discernment. If we are easily inclined to discouragement, for example, we need to watch for this during our prayers. Self-knowledge, then, is essential for effective discernment.

9

The Discerning Community

Welcome one another, therefore, just as Christ has welcomed you,
for the glory of God. . . . May the God of hope fill
you with all joy and peace in believing, so that you may
abound in hope by the power of the Holy Spirit.
ROMANS 15:7, 13

We *never discern in isolation; we discern in community. Every* significant choice we make reflects the fact that we are profoundly interconnected with the lives of others. Our decisions inevitably affect others but are also affected by the choices that others make. It is only appropriate that we are accountable to others in our choices; others need to be able to challenge us and confirm whether what we believe to be God's will is truly of God. We need the wisdom and counsel of others.

But just being in community does not necessarily make for good discernment. The communal demands and expectations can actually undermine authentic discernment. We are faced with a twofold challenge. First, how can we free one another to choose well so that our choices are not inordinately influenced by the weight of communal expectations? Second, how can the community genuinely participate in our decision-making process in a way that encourages good choices?

The Challenge of Discernment in Community

The problem is straightforward: people often choose poorly because they are overly conscious of the expectations of their community. Many Christians are seemingly incapable of listening to God in times of choice because their spouse, parents, friends, coworkers or fellow church members do not free them to choose well.

I grieved when I heard a man in midlife say that he had no certainty that God was calling him back to the mission field after a furlough, but he was nevertheless returning simply because he could not face his home church with the news that he was not returning. All too often people cannot hear God in their decision-making because the expectations of the community are so loud and overpowering.

For others the challenge is to hear God in the face of parental expectations. The desire to please parents can be so overwhelming that they cannot listen to God. Their self-esteem is locked to their parents' opinions. All they can see and hear is what their parents want. Parents often get caught in the trap of playing the role of parent long after their child should have become an adult accountable to the heavenly Father and no longer to an earthly parent.

Yet at the same time we must emphasize the vital place of the community in the discernment process. We make our own decisions, but we are never alone in the end. We live in communities. And one of the most wonderful gifts we can give one another is the time, space and encouragement to choose well.

The ideal is to be a community of faith where women and men are able to hear God and encouraged to be open to the prompting of God. But we can become such a community only if we are conscious of the dangers that are inherent in community. We can help others only if we are alert to how our "help" can actually be an obstacle to discernment.

We need the encouragement of the community in the choices we make, and communities need to be settings where members of the community can choose well. Each of us will have the opportunity to enable another to make a choice and to choose well. The challenge, then, is to nurture the qualities and characteristics within our communities that encourage good discernment. Whether it is with respect to the role of a clearness committee, a spiritual director or the community as a whole, the issue is fundamentally the same: how can we free one another and enable one another to choose well?

Behind these reflections are two simple questions. How can you and I be a means of encouragement and support to others who are making decisions? And how can you and I find the help we need when we are making a choice? Each of us is regularly placed in a context or relationship where we have the opportunity to help another. Some are pastors, parents, counselors or spiritual directors—people in positions of trust and authority. Others are in situations where friends or colleagues are making a choice. But we are all in a position, many times over, to be of help to others.

We all frequently recognize that in the midst of a choice we must make, we are alone and need the help of others. Naturally, we need to know how to get the help we need and avoid those elements in community that will keep us from discerning well.

The question, then, is pertinent to all of us: how can we be communities that encourage and foster discernment?

The Resolve to Free Others to Hear God

First and foremost is a simple principle: Discerning communities

believe that each Christian has the capacity to respond personally to God. While new believers or young people may need a
greater measure of guidance, we must be cautious and realize
that our goal is never to control. Maturity in Christian faith
requires that each person learn to listen to God for himself or
herself.

We will make mistakes; we will make choices poorly. But often
the only way to learn is through those very mistakes. If parents
protect their teenager, never letting the young person make
choices that the parents deem less than wise, the teen will never
become an adult who responds to God.

Similarly, with proper coaching even a new Christian can
begin to respond to the prompting of the Spirit and learn to take
the time and space to discern well in times of choice. Yes, good
spiritual counsel is still needed (for all of us, actually). And yes,
we may need to raise cautions, express concerns and challenge
motives—but then we all need this kind of input.

We must free one another to choose. We need to enable each
individual to respond to God for themselves and resist the
temptation to be God to one another or assume that we know
what God's will is for our neighbor.

The problem is that many people find a degree of satisfaction
through their capacity to control others. They cannot function
within community except by subtle (or less than subtle) manipulation and a spirit of judgmentalism. They are threatened by the
freedom of others, and so they make their expectations known.
In the more extreme cases they use emotional blackmail to get
their way. We have all met them—parents who suggest, subtly or
otherwise, that if we love them we will fulfill their expectations,
or church leaders (pastors or elders) who suggest that if we love
the Lord we will fulfill their expectations by being present for
some meeting or taking on some responsibility.

These people invariably equate their will with the will of God. They are sure that others do not need to discern, for the will of God is clear. They know it and are happy to be the conduit by which *we* know it! They cannot handle the word *no*. Their self-esteem is wrapped up in getting others to fulfill their expectations. A "no" for them is rejection, so they will use subtle manipulation to get their way. They will not let others think and discern for themselves.

The tragedy is that they often get away with it. People buy into this emotional blackmail, often out of a genuine desire to please another but as often as not because they too fear rejection. They fear the consequences of not fulfilling the expectation of the other. And the consequence is that authentic discernment is virtually impossible.

We can be discerning communities only if we make it clear and state it often that we believe in the capacity of each Christian to hear the voice of God and that we do not equate the voice of God with the expectations we have of one another. And we do need to say this often. We need to call one another to account when we hear words or subtle statements that restrict others' freedom to listen to God. We must be alert to the spirit of judgmentalism that destroys individual discernment. We cannot afford to even hint that we are god to one another.

Behind all of this, of course, is the assumption that we are learning together what it means to discern well. Of course we cannot cut people adrift to choose entirely on their own. No. We discern in community. But—and this is the critical point—we must, as members of communities, free one another to listen to God.

This does not mean that we cannot make suggestions; it is merely that we probably serve one another best when we avoid using the word *should*—as in "You should be here" or "You should do that." We can *suggest* to one another the need to consider a particular possibility—but always in a spirit of openness and freedom.

St. John of the Cross in his "Living Flame of Love" (3.29-67) says that inadequate spiritual directors (actually those who are not just inadequate but dangerous) are those who (1) presume to control or determine how an individual should live his or her life and (2) assume that the person they are directing will experience God in the same way they did. The same principles apply to the community as a whole. We are a discerning community only if each is enabled to listen to God.

An Atmosphere of Honesty and Self-Knowledge

Further, we can be discerning communities only if we can nurture a social environment of honesty with God, with one another and with ourselves. Few things so effectively undermine good discernment as inauthenticity. We live with masks before one another and consequently never learn to be honest with God.

There are certainly different ways in which an environment of authenticity can be nurtured in our homes, our communities of faith and our places of work. It will require, for example, that we free one another to be different. We can delight in what makes each person unique and celebrate the diversity reflected in different personalities, different abilities and different contributions.

Such an environment also requires that we free one another to express our desires and be honest about what we want, what is important to us and what our values are. If we are dishonest about our desires, always spiritualizing away what we want or deferring to the desires and wants of another, we ultimately live a lie. We are no longer authentic. And the time will come when we do not *know* what we want. Children whose parents discourage them from expressing their own desires, or wives (more often than not it is the wife) who always defer to the desires of their husbands, or people in the workplace who are always listening to others in order to find out how they will express their convictions or desires eventually lose the ability to express themselves from the depths of their beings. Communities that encourage authenticity free people to express their desires.

Members of these communities free one another to express their feelings as well. As stated earlier, we cannot discern well unless we are in touch with our feelings. This naturally means that we are honest about what we are feeling. But if our communities—families, local assemblies of believers or places of work—discourage us from honestly expressing our feelings or acknowledging them, it will inevitably mean that we cannot discern well.

This does not mean that every time we are angry we yell and behave violently, or that every time we are discouraged we walk around with ashes on our heads! But it does mean that we do not lie about our feelings and that we allow one another to have feelings of anger when these are appropriate, or be discouraged when there has been a setback, or feel anxiety or fear when there is uncertainty or something that threatens our well-being. Only as we are honest about our feelings—especially the feelings of desolation—can we urge one another to avoid choices *in* desolation.

Finally, of course, we are a community of discernment only if our honesty means that we refuse to flatter one another. We do not lie to each other; we do not say that people are good at something when they are not. We realize that nothing is gained by false consolation or fabricated encouragement. We have learned, in the words of the apostle James, to let our yes be yes and our no no. It is not that we are cruel or insensitive. It does mean, however, that people in time can learn to depend on us and know that when we speak our words are an honest reflection of what we see, what we want and why we think there is hope in a particular situation.

Whether in our differences, our desires or our feelings, the fundamental point here is that we encourage honesty and self-knowledge. Only then can we be a community that enables and encourages its members to discern well.

An Environment of Mutual Encouragement and Hope

People are sometimes so overwhelmed and discouraged by the circumstances in which they are making a choice that the very emotional weight of the choice undermines their capacity to choose well. We cannot discern well without hope. Discouragement darkens the mind, shuts out our capacity to see the possibilities before us and disables us from responding to God's grace. This is why one of the greatest gifts we can give to one another is encouragement. A good spiritual director has the capacity to bring encouragement and hope—sometimes just by empathic listening, other times by pointing out that circumstances are not as bad as we think they are, or perhaps by reminding us of God's faithfulness in the past or of our capacity to make good choices in the past.

One of the ways we encourage is through empathic listening. This is often the greatest gift we give another—the gift of not speaking. Frequently when someone speaks about their circumstances, the problems they are facing or the choices they feel compelled to make, we feel we need to come up with a wise word or some kind of good counsel. But the first thing that is needed is an attentive ear.

You can ask questions that enable you to understand the circumstances of the other person. But be careful that you do not reply prematurely to their questions or to what you see of their circumstances—if for no other reason than you have yet to hear the whole story. In the end, though, it is important to recognize that the act of listening is not merely a means of getting the information you need to give wise counsel; in itself it is an act of service that brings hope and so makes discernment possible.

We also encourage by affirming where we see God at work in each other. This is one of the great gifts that a spiritual director gives. I particularly enjoy the story of Eli and Samuel (1 Sam 3). Samuel keeps thinking that he hears Eli calling him; finally Eli suggests that what Samuel is hearing is the voice of God.

The danger, of course, is that we may identify what we want the other to hear or respond to. But can we not with joy acknowledge where we see the sign of the Spirit in the life of another?

We do not need to force our opinions on another. We can gently suggest that perhaps what they take to be the voice of another, or a voice that interrupts, is really the voice of God. We can acknowledge where we see the hand of God without being prescriptive.

Perhaps we can suggest that what they think of as a distraction in prayer is really something that they need to acknowledge and respond to. Or we can raise the possibility that the people who seem so difficult or the views that stand as opposition are really the hand of God. Just as Habakkuk had to accept the reality of God working through the Assyrians, even so we need to see that God is often at work in ways that may be quite painful rather than pleasant. It is still the work of God.

When someone is overcome with hectic activity or noise, the expectations of others or the size of their problems, we can urge them to find the space and time to hear the still small voice of God. When we do, we bring hope; we encourage.

We also encourage by enjoying and blessing one another. When we delight in each other, take joy in each other, we bless, and this is a powerful means of encouraging a friend, colleague or young person. As a parent, for example, I cannot free my sons to discern for themselves unless I bless them—delight in them quite apart from whether they fulfill my expectations. And to the extent that I do, I know that I strengthen each of them in his capacity to be his own person before God.

It takes time to nurture a community of authenticity and discernment. It takes time to develop the trust necessary for the honest and openness such a community requires. But it is time well invested. For a discerning community has a tremendous capacity to free and enable people to mature in faith and discernment.

10

Patience with God

I have calmed and quieted my soul,
like a weaned child with its mother;
my soul is like the weaned child that is with me.
PSALM 131:2

Be still before the LORD, and wait patiently for him.
PSALM 37:7

A *basic premise of this reflective study is that God still speaks.*
God's love and faithfulness is intimate and immediate. God is
Father and Shepherd, guide and friend. But there is another
side to God that must be affirmed: the Lord of the heavens is
also transcendent and holy, majestic in his otherness. And God
is both wise and free.

We need to consider afresh these last two characteristics—
the wisdom and the freedom of God. A renewed appreciation
of these attributes of God gives a different dimension to our
prayers and therefore to our discernment. It shapes our understanding of the reality of suffering on the one hand and
the silence of God on the other. In both respects we discover
that the heart of faith is learning to have patience with God,
and this is captured simply in the exhortation of Psalm 37:7:

"Be still before the LORD, and wait patiently for him."

The Reality of Suffering

The prophet Habakkuk, in the Old Testament prophetic book that bears his name, is portrayed as a man who sincerely desired that which is righteous, just and true. He also surely loved the people of God, and so grieved when he saw Israel oppressed. And his love of justice led him to cry out to God when he was bewildered by the activity of God: "Why, O God," he asked, "do the righteous suffer and the wicked prosper? Why do you make me look at injustice? Why do you, O God, tolerate wrong?" (see Hab 1).

Habakkuk asks bold but honest questions. Here we find no pious sentimentality, no superspiritual type always wearing a happy face. Rather we find a man who would be genuinely perplexed by such lines from religious songs as "Every day with Jesus is sweeter than the day before." For in his perspective some days with the Lord were uncertain, disturbing and dark.

I do not believe I am oversimplifying in saying that God's answer is "Trust me with this one, Habakkuk; I know what I am doing." Of course that is always God's answer to us. We are all called to trust God at each point in our pilgrimage. The whole of the Christian experience is to be lived from a position of trust in the living God. But it is at the confusing moments, when things do not seem right or true or good, that our trust is tested. And nothing will test our faith like difficulty, especially when we do not understand the need for the pain—when it makes no sense to us.

There is an ancient counsel that we must keep ever before us: God works in mysterious ways—mysterious to us, that is. He confounds the wisdom of the wise. He uses the weak things of this world as the means of glorifying himself on the earth. And he often works through our adversity, even our failure, to fulfill his good and perfect purposes.

This in itself should not surprise us, since God chose to glorify himself and bring healing to the created order through the death of his Son. The cross stands forever as a sign that God works through death, difficulty and suffering. But we are surprised. It seems as though difficulty and obstacles in our lives consistently take us off guard, leave us bewildered and certain that something has gone wrong. It may be that something is wrong. But it could also be that God allows the wrong because of his greater purposes. Habakkuk came to the sobering realization that the Assyrians, the terrible and wicked army that came against God's people, were the hand of God.

Many contemporary Christian communities seem to embrace the basic premise that the purposes of God are simple: to make us comfortable and happy. While there is no doubt that the ultimate purpose of God is that our joy would be complete, we often confuse this to mean that God wants us to be comfortable and at ease. This notion naturally undermines the ability of Christians to discern the will of a God who works through difficulty, suffering and even failure. The bias for comfort tends to blind us to a whole dimension of God's work. That is why there are few things so critical to discernment as good theology.

This inclination to seek comfort and expect comfort is a recent phenomenon. Our forefathers and mothers knew full well that the kingdom of God would come through adversity, and we have tremendous testimonies to the grace of God in difficulty—tribulation that was not understood but was accepted with grace. This is expressed well in the hymn of the eighteenth-century poet William Cowper:

> God moves in a mysterious way
> His wonders to perform;

He plants his footsteps in the sea,
 and rides upon the storm.

Ye fearful saints, fresh courage take;
 the clouds ye so much dread
Are big with mercy, and shall break
 in blessings on your head.

Judge not the Lord by feeble sense,
 But trust Him for his grace;
Behind a frowning providence
 He hides a smiling face.

His purposes will ripen fast,
 Unfolding every hour:
The bud may have a bitter taste,
 But sweet will be the flower.

Blind unbelief is sure to err,
 And scan His work in vain:
God is His own interpreter,
 And He will make it plain.

"God is His own interpreter": and so we hear the admonition "Judge not the Lord by feeble sense." We are called to trust God, and this trust is foundational to effective discernment. Without it we will always be blinded to the purposes of God by our own wisdom, our own limited perspective and experience, our own "feeble sense."

Discernment is not easy when we are under the stress of crisis, difficulty and opposition. When we are being criticized or opposed or even hated, or when we are wondering whether the route we have chosen is the right one given the difficulty we have encountered, discernment can be daunting. The pain and confusion of the moment make discernment formidable. We feel as though it is impossible to know what God wants or even what we want. We want to run from the trouble, but we also want to do what is right. We know very well that the hurt of criticism or the fear of pain and suffering can easily cloud our minds and undermine our ability to hear the voice of God.

At such points I have found hymns like Cowper's "God Moves in a Mysterious Way" to be a source of great comfort. As noted earlier, we cannot discern in desolation, only in consolation. And the mere reminder that our difficulty and pain is not a surprise to God is itself a tremendous source of reassurance. I may still be perplexed; I still may ask God why he would allow such a development. But the knowledge that God works through pain, difficulty and defeat is a source of comfort. Only in this understanding can we come to the task of discernment with some measure of freedom.

Habakkuk moved from perplexity to profound peace. His discernment arose from faith and gracious acceptance of the purposes of God. He determined to rejoice in God even if things did not go well (Hab 3:17-19). The reference point for his peace was God, not his circumstances, however severe or perplexing his situation.

So we may make a rational judgment that something is right or wrong. This is an essential part of discernment—rational consideration of the circumstances of our lives. But that in itself is only the first step and in no way determines our response. Afterward we need to discern whether the harder, less logical way is nevertheless the way God would have us go. This is essentially what happened to our Lord in Gethsemane. He accepted the wrong.

Thomas Green has put it well when he writes,

The mind's judgment about right and wrong is not decisive
by itself in determining how we respond. . . . There is no doubt,
it seems to me, that Calvary was "wrong," the work of evil men
in a corrupt institutional situation, and yet Jesus discerned
that it was the Father's will for him that he submit "like a lamb
led to the slaughter."[1]

The fact that something is wrong in the situation we face does
not preclude discernment. We must still discern our response,
what is best in the Lord in this situation. We will face unjust
situations and circumstances where there is plenty of evidence
of evil. In those situations discernment may be difficult because
of the pressure, uncertainty and inner turmoil that come with
opposition and even the hatred of others, the fear that others
will harm us or those we love. But though difficult, discernment
is crucial. We must find the peace of God by turning from anger,
fear, disappointment and discouragement, and in peace discern
what is best—what is the good and perfect will of God for us in
this situation. We can then respond with strength.

This perspective is based on the simple assumption that we
must distinguish between God's permissive will and God's perfect will. God may allow suffering and difficulty. But this is not
God's perfect will for us. God does not delight in our suffering,
but God will allow difficulty as the means by which he fulfills his
good and perfect will in us and in the world. Therefore we can
freely distinguish and recognize that not everything that happens in the world reflects the perfect will of God. Many things
happen that are wrong and evil and a violation of God's will. The
fact that they happen does not make them God's will. God
allowed them, but he does not necessarily choose them.

But in any circumstance we can find joy and be grateful. We
do not thank God for all things, for God is only the author of

good. But even in the darkest hour, God is with us; his presence can be discerned. And for this, and for the signs of his goodness in even the most difficult of times, we can be thankful.

Which leads us to consider another dimension of discernment.

The Silence of God

The summer of 1989 was a difficult one for me and my family. My wife and I had resigned from a previous position confident that we were doing what was right at the time. We also had reason, apart from a simple confidence in God's provision, to believe that another position would be available to us within a few months. I accepted an interim pastoral position while waiting for this prospect to be finalized. But nothing happened. I wrote letters and received polite responses that left me perplexed and uncertain. I began to doubt my previous decision, wondering whether I had deluded myself.

As the weeks and months went by, my turmoil grew. I remember thinking that God must have misplaced my file somewhere and forgotten that I was married, with two children, and in need of a job! Days of prayer and discernment led nowhere because there seemed to be nothing to discern. There was one job offer, but at the time we felt no peace to accept it.

After about four months a guest preacher came to our church, Roberta Hestenes of Eastern College. I picked her up on Sunday morning at her hotel, and as we drove to the church she asked first about the church and then about me. I would have liked to describe myself as someone who knew who he was and where he was going. But I had to confess—rather uneasily—that I was between jobs, in transition, and was actually facing the possibility of being unemployed in the near future.

She listened carefully and asked a few leading questions to

clarify the nature of my situation. But her response in the end was actually rather curt. At least I felt it was. As we drove into the church parking lot she said, "Gordon, this will not hurt you, you know."

I knew she was right. And I knew that what she had said was God's word to me. God was under no obligation to guide me and direct me any sooner than he needed to. At the time I had a position; I was employed in a ministry that I was thoroughly enjoying. In peace I only needed to wait for God.

The next day I was scheduled to have lunch with another individual who happened to be in town, Robert Ferris. I had known him for some time, but we had not seen each other for a couple of years. Naturally, we caught up on developments; Bob wanted to know why I had resigned from my former position and where I thought this would lead. Again I felt the inner discomfort—probably nothing more than the discomfort of a male ego that cannot respond with certainty and decisiveness—as I again noted that I was "in transition," waiting for something to open up.

Bob's response was about as short as that of Dr. Hestenes's. He suggested that I read Psalm 131, which I did later that day:

My heart is not proud, O LORD,
　My eyes are not haughty;
I do not concern myself with great matters
　or things too wonderful for me.
But I have stilled and quieted my soul;
　like a weaned child with its mother,
　like a weaned child is my soul within me.

O Israel, put your hope in the LORD
　both now and forevermore. (NIV)

Again, Bob's suggestion was God's word to me. The encounter with these two individuals, and their freedom to speak, was a turning point. I needed to turn from anxiety and fear, turmoil and frustration. My greatest need was to wait in peace upon God, who for the time was silent (though I saw signs of his presence).

These individuals came into my life with encouragement and admonition. Yet when it came to what I felt was my most crucial need, direction from God, there was silence. Direction was not my greatest need, of course. My most critical need was to let God be God, and to trust him and wait for him.

God cannot be rushed. Discernment takes time, as much time as God deems necessary. The Lord will not abandon us or forget us or lose our file! A sense of hurry or panic undermines our ability to recognize his voice. Our deadlines and timetables are often artificial and often need to be set aside so that we can attend to God, allowing God to speak to us in his time and according to his timetable.

If we trust God, his timing as well as his wisdom, we are free to discern. Another hymn puts it well:

If thou but suffer God to guide thee
And hope in Him through all thy ways,
He'll give thee strength, whate'er betide thee,
And bear thee through the evil days;
Who trusts in God's unchanging love
Builds on the rock that naught can move.

Only be still, and wait His leisure
In cheerful hope, with heart content
To take whate'er they Father's pleasure
And all-discerning love hath sent;
Nor doubt our inmost wants are known

To Him who chose us for His own.

Sing, pray, and keep His ways unswerving;
So do thine own part faithfully,
And trust His Word—though undeserving,
Thou yet shalt find it true for thee;
God never yet forsook at need
The soul that trusted Him indeed.

(Georg Neumark, 1621-1681; trans. Catherine Winkworth)

Some time ago I heard a sermon that left a lasting impression on me. It was about David, the king of Israel. The preacher noted that the greatest enemy and opponent in David's life was Saul, who hounded him for ten years or more. I was impressed by this sermon in part because I had recently gone through a time of intense difficulty as a pastor, with severe opposition to my ministry. During that time several sincere Christians had reminded me of David and Goliath. One gave me a tape of a sermon that described the great faith of David, who because he trusted God was able to destroy his enemy with one stone, and said that if we had similar faith "the Goliaths of our lives would fall and we would go forward in victory." Well, the Goliaths of my life had gone nowhere despite all the faith I could muster.

The sermon on David and Saul was liberating for me because it was a reminder that Goliath was an exception for David; the norm was Saul. For ten years or more David was on the run from Saul. He had no permanent address, being forced to live in caves. His friendship with Jonathan was destroyed by Saul. Yet on the run he composed some of the greatest poetry we find in the Psalter. In fear for his life, he nevertheless acted with integrity when he had the opportunity to kill Saul, refusing to raise his hand against the anointed one of God. He chose to wait for God. He chose patience with God rather than taking things into his own hands.

Few perspectives are so critical to the task of discernment as letting God be God, choosing to live within the limitations and even the difficulty that are either provided by God or allowed by God. This is the essence of faith, of course, and this faith is the most fundamental prerequisite for discernment. Let us then be still and patient with God.

Epilogue

If there is one image, word or concept that captures what discernment in a time of decisions is all about, it is surely *receptivity*. We tend to think of authentic spirituality as being anything from faithful adherence to doctrines and creeds to active involvement in church affairs or church work. In themselves these are good, of course. But they have the potential to draw us away from the fundamental question: Are we open to the Lord, to the depths of our being? Is there first and foremost an abandonment of our selves, our whole selves, to the love and goodness of God? Are we truly open to what he has for us?

This receptivity seeks his grace for today, refusing to clutch the hurts and pain of yesterday. It turns from the "if only" of regret and with gratitude explores fresh options for today. But this receptivity is also a humble acceptance of ourselves—without apology, without comparison with others and without pretense or fear. I must be open to God—radically, to the depth and root of my being. But it is as myself that I am open to God—all that I am. I do not offer him what I wish I was, but what I am; I do not offer him something I compare with others, but only what I have. I present myself to him as a living sacrifice (Rom 12:1). Only as I do so do I know authentic humility—a receptivity that accepts self and as self lets God be God.

We have a strange idea that God does not really care for us, does not really like us and certainly does not take seriously who we are and what we want. So it is difficult for us to really believe that God wants to give us the desires of our hearts. But—and this is the point—God cannot grant us the fullness of his grace to sanctify the whole of our lives, including our desires, unless we have a fundamental receptivity to him.

Receptivity also means that we relinquish control. God must remain God. And receptivity means that we accept the initiatives as well as the timing of God, trusting ourselves to both his wisdom and his goodness.

We will know the grace of God and recognize his voice in times of decision, gaining increasing confidence in our choices, as we grow in a fundamental openness and receptivity to God.

Notes

Chapter 1: Dancing with God

[1]Ernest Larkin, *Silent Presence: Discernment as Process and Problem* (Denville, N.J.: Dimension, 1981), p. 28.

[2]Ibid., pp. 58-59.

Chapter 2: Seeking the Best

[1]*The Spiritual Exercises of St. Ignatius,* ed. Louis J. Puhl (Chicago: Loyola University Press, 1975). This reference and all additional parenthetical references are to paragraph numbers.

[2]A. W. Tozer, "How the Lord Leads," *The Alliance Weekly* 92 (January 2, 1957): 2.

[3]Tad Dunne, *Spiritual Mentoring: Guiding People Through Spiritual Exercises to Life Decisions* (San Francisco: HarperSanFrancisco, 1991), p. 167.

[4]Reynolds Price, *A Whole New Life* (New York: Atheneum, 1994).

[5]John Wesley, "The Witness of the Spirit," in *The Works of John Wesley,* ed. Albert C. Outler (Nashville: Abingdon, 1984), 1:269.

[6]Ibid.

Chapter 3: The Personal Foundations of Discernment

[1]Tozer, "How the Lord Leads," p. 2.

[2]Klaus Bockmuehl, *Listening to the God Who Speaks* (Colorado Springs, Colo.: Helmers & Howard, 1990), p. 125.

Chapter 4: The Peace of God

[1]A. B. Simpson, *The Holy Spirit* (reprint Harrisburg, Penn.: Christian Publications, 1960), p. 181.

[2]My analysis of Ignatius's rules follows the perspective and insights of Thomas H. Green, S.J.

[3]As noted earlier, references are to paragraph numbers in the *Spiritual Exercises.*

[4]Thomas H. Green, *Weeds Among the Wheat* (Notre Dame, Ind.: Ave Maria, 1984), p. 108.

[5]Ibid., p. 136.

[6]Ibid., pp. 137-41.

Chapter 5: An Intentional Approach to Decision-Making
[1]Parker Palmer, "The Clearness Committee: The Way of Discernment," *Weavings* 3, no. 4 (July-August 1988): 38.

Chapter 6: People of Discernment
[1]Larkin, *Silent Presence,* p. 10.
[2]A. W. Tozer, *The Pursuit of God* (Harrisburg, Penn.: Christian Publications, 1948), pp. 66-67.
[3]John Carmody, *Re-examining Conscience* (New York: Seabury, 1982), p. 18.
[4]Ibid., pp. 18-19.
[5]Teresa of Ávila, *The Interior Castle,* in *The Collected Works of St. Teresa of Ávila,* trans. Kieran Kavanaugh and Otilio Rodriguez (Washington, D.C.: Institute of Carmelite Studies Publications, 1980), 2:291-92.
[6]Thomas Merton, *Spiritual Direction and Meditation* (Collegeville, Minn.: Liturgical Press, 1960), pp. 35-38.
[7]Larkin, *Silent Presence,* pp. 7-8.
[8]Tozer, *Pursuit of God,* p. 114.

Chapter 7: A Discernment Notebook
[1]Gary Friesen, *Decision Making and the Will of God* (Portland, Ore.: Multnomah Press, 1980), pp. 120-21.
[2]Bockmuehl, *Listening to the God Who Speaks,* p. 51.
[3]Friesen, *Decision Making and the Will of God,* pp. 133-34.
[4]James Fowler, *Becoming Christian, Becoming Adult* (San Francisco: Harper & Row, 1984), p. 103.
[5]Terry Muck, "The Back Page," *Leadership* 11, no. 2 (Spring 1990): 146.
[6]Ronald Barnes, "Dreams in Spiritual Direction: Help or Distraction?" in *The Christian Ministry of Spiritual Direction,* ed. David L. Fleming (St. Louis: Review for Religious, 1988), pp. 381-99.

Chapter 8: Blocks to Discernment
[1]Margaret Goldsbury, "Diminishing God's Handiwork: Blocks to Discernment," *The Way Supplement: The Place of Discernment,* no. 64 (Spring 1989): 81.
[2]Ibid., p. 83.

Chapter 10: Patience with God
[1]Thomas H. Green, *Darkness in the Marketplace* (Notre Dame, Ind.: Ave Maria, 1981), p. 43 n.

For Further Reading

Bockmuehl, Klaus. *Listening to the God Who Speaks.* Colorado Springs, Colo.: Helmers & Howard, 1990.

Carmody, John. *Re-examining Conscience.* New York: Seabury Press, 1982.

Dunne, Tad. *Spiritual Mentoring: Guiding People Through Spiritual Exercises to Life Decisions.* San Francisco: HarperSanFrancisco, 1991.

English, John J. *Spiritual Freedom.* Guelph, Ont.: Loyola House, 1979.

Fowler, James W. *Becoming Christian, Becoming Adult.* San Francisco: Harper & Row, 1984.

Friesen, Garry. *Decision Making and the Will of God.* Portland, Ore.: Multnomah Press, 1980.

Green, Thomas H. *Darkness in the Marketplace.* Notre Dame, Ind.: Ave Maria, 1981.

————. *Weeds Among the Wheat.* Notre Dame, Ind.: Ave Maria, 1984.

Ignatius of Loyola. *The Spiritual Exercises of St. Ignatius.* Trans. Louis J. Puhl. Chicago: Loyola University Press, 1975.

Johnson, Ben Campbell. *Discerning God's Will.* Louisville, Ky.: Westminster/John Knox, 1990.

Larkin, Ernest E. *Silent Presence: Discernment as Process and Problem.* Denville, N.J.: Dimension Books, 1981.

Lewis, C. S. *The Screwtape Letters.* London: Geoffrey Bles, 1942.

Merton, Thomas. *No Man Is an Island.* New York: Harcourt Brace Jovanovich, 1955.

————. *Spiritual Direction and Meditation.* Collegeville, Minn.: Liturgical Press, 1960.

O'Sullivan, Michael J. "Trust Your Feelings, but Use Your Head: Discernment and the Psychology of Decision Making." *Studies in the Spirituality of Jesuits* 22, no. 4 (September 1990).

Palmer, Parker. "The Clearness Committee: The Way of Discernment." *Weavings* 3, no. 4 (July-August 1988): 37-40.

Wolff, Pierre. *Discernment: The Art of Choosing Well.* Liguori, Mo.: Triumph, 1993.

Wuellner, Flora. "Were Not Our Hearts Burning Within Us?" *Weavings* 10, no. 6 (November-December 1995).